A MENTORING CLASSIC

First published in 1983 as *Mentors and Proteges*, this book presents the ins and outs of the "new mentoring" now enjoyed by millions worldwide. Using updated case studies, anecdotes of well-known people, and her counseling and consulting experiences, Dr. Phillips-Jones presents a learnable, enjoyable approach for giving and receiving effective mentoring.

"Linda has been instrumental in creating an extremely successful high potential development program within Hewlett-Packard and Agilent. Her insights, depth of knowledge, and ability to help people use them are remarkable."

— Patricia A. Chapman, manager,
Agilent Technologies

"This is a wonderful book. It's extremely valuable and needed in corporate America."

— Sally Alvarez, manager,
Enron Corporation

"Dr. Phillips-Jones' materials are insightful and match the values of our company. Unlike most resource materials, I couldn't put them down."

— John Hansen, manager,
Restaurants Unlimited

The New Mentors & Proteges

Linda Phillips-Jones, Ph.D.

Other Titles by Linda Phillips-Jones:

Mentors and Proteges
The Mentor's Guide
The Mentee's Guide
The Mentoring Program Coordinator's Guide
The Mentoring Program Design Package

(with G. Brian Jones)
Men Have Feelings, Too!
A Fight to the Better End

Cover design by Tracy Nino

To Brian, who not only believes in—but lives— excellent mentoring

Contents

Preface

In 1977, when I wrote my dissertation on mentoring, and in 1983, when I wrote the first version of this book, mentoring was *not* a household word. People were skeptical about the notion that mentoring could be planned and managed and that mentees could have a say in the process.

Yet, despite strong resistance, the age-old concept of mentoring was changing, and the mentoring movement was creating a lot of excitement and gaining strength.

Over the next few years, this *"new mentoring"* continued to evolve. I revised the book in 1993 and 1997, calling it *The New Mentors and Proteges*. Now, almost 18 years after the first edition, mentoring has changed even more. I've decided to update and enhance this volume one last time.

Today, newspapers, magazines, dictionaries, and radio and t.v. public service announcements regularly include the terms *mentor* and *mentoring*. Hundreds of websites focus on the topic, and thousands of others at least mention it. Mentoring finally is a household word.

Today's mentor-mentee combinations differ from the forms they took earlier. In addition to pairs, mentoring alliances are

trios, quartets, and larger groups, sometimes called mentoring circles. Young mentors often mentor older mentees. Partnerships have new rules, expectations and
activities.

A mentoring industry has developed
complete with hundreds of consultants, at
least one national association, and an extensive array of mentoring books, training
materials, articles, newsletters, theses, dissertations, tapes, videos, and on-line resources. Mentors and mentees are learning
mentoring skills and procedures in creative
new ways.

As a licensed psychologist in private
practice for two decades, I've learned how
successful mentoring works and the impact
it can have. *An effective mentor can help a
protege move from mediocre to excellent performance, from weariness to excitement and
passion—even when the protege hasn't had
much success before.*

In consulting with private corporations
and not-for-profit institutions, I've seen that
mentoring has extraordinary value for individuals—as well as for organizations. Today
it's the rare entity that *isn't* trying to improve the formal or informal mentoring of its
people.

Some things *haven't* changed since
1983. When young or inexperienced persons
learn about mentoring, they're usually eager
to be part of it. Most good mentors still don't

believe they're doing much for their mentees.

An ideal term hasn't been adopted for
the persons helped by mentors. The most
powerful help a mentor can give is still believing in the individual and encouraging him
or her to succeed.

A group of individuals will always
remain who think the mentoring process
can't be planned or formalized and should
only happen naturally.

Because of these continuing truths and
viewpoints, much of the content of this edition is the same as that of the earlier versions.

Another thing that remains is my deep
gratitude for my own mentors: high school
teacher John Beatty; professors Bernie Anderson, Chuck Healy, Mel Barlow, and
Warren Schmidt; spiritual mentor Diane
Kennedy; adopted mom-mentor Cele Becker;
my terrific husband-mentor and colleague,
Brian Jones, and my ultimate mentor,
Christ. Each dramatically improved my life
during our initial encounters and, in fact,
continue to impact my life today.

I've changed names in the book except
for those of well-known public figures and a
few others who gave me permission to include their stories.

Several people deserve thanks for
their help with this updated edition. Dozens
of colleagues especially Brian Jones, Pat

Chapman, Lynn Erickson, Kathy Kram, Lisa Lion Wolfe, Susan Byrne, and Kathleen Borges continue to teach me about mentoring.

Graphic designer Tracy Nino created the book cover. Banta Book Group provided excellent production work. Vicki Bahnsen, The Mentoring Group's administrative manager, added her never-ending encouragement plus creative and professional touches to the entire writing and publishing process. Cele and Linda Becker, Lynda and Jack Murphy, Laurie Schell, Stan and Nancy Zabka, and Nancy Bennett remain my biased and avid cheerleaders.

You, reader, encourage me greatly because of your interest in mentoring. If you haven't already, I urge you to make mentoring a part of your life.

Linda Phillips-Jones
www.mentoringgroup.com

1

The New
Mentors and Proteges

*Instead of waiting for someone to take
you under his wing, go out and find a
good wing to climb under.*

—Dave Thomas
Founder of Wendy's

If you're considering, entering, enjoying, or struggling with a mentoring relationship, get comfortable, because this book is for you. Consider it your personal handbook for understanding and personalizing a powerful strategy that will help you succeed.

The first part of the book will help you become a highly effective mentee or protege. You'll learn how to find and manage the mentoring you need.

Later in the book, we'll switch gears, and you'll see how to properly mentor others and how to help other would-be proteges find mentoring that's right for them.

Mentoring has actually been around as long as people have. This book will show you how it's been *modernized* by your peers to increase skills, widen and deepen perspectives, increase self-confidence, open doors, avoid errors, save time and energy, and otherwise enhance their careers and lives in general.

Although mentoring happened through the centuries, the modern variety began in the 1970s and 1980s. Particularly in the U.S., thousands of what I call "pioneer proteges" did what was then unheard of. They actively sought and negotiated formal relationships with mentors, who were more than a little surprised to be approached.

Although this group of pioneer proteges boldly initiated relationships for the first time, most mentors still did the leading in those relationships. Many still insisted on calling all the shots.

Today's mentors and proteges and the relationships they share are different from all of these predecessors. Here's how.

1. Today's mentees are managing their mentoring relationships.

Mentees are taking more of the lead in their mentoring partnerships. They're seeking and negotiating arrangements with mentors, and they're managing the direction and details of those relationships.

Mentees realize their new mentoring relationships are likely to be shorter than the ones of the past. Most realize that a different protocol or etiquette now exists in mentoring relationships, although many aren't exactly sure what it is or how to follow it. They wonder, how *do* you actually manage a mentoring relationship?

2. The new mentees are seeking multiple mentors.

The new mentees are discovering that investing energy in *one* mentor isn't wise, and in fact it's naive to expect one person to provide everything.

They're setting personal and career goals different from those of their parents and even from the goals they themselves valued earlier. They're acquiring two or more mentors to help them work on the same or different goals.

3. The new proteges are seeking mentors for all areas of their lives.

Years ago, people sought wise advisors including family members to teach them intellectual, emotional, spiritual, physical, and social truths and skills. In the 1980s and 1990s, proteges searched for mentors mainly for career help.

Now, proteges are again pursuing mentors for all areas of their lives. A difference is that they find separate mentors for the different areas.

Today's mentees recognize that money and exciting careers are important but not everything. They're seeking experts to help them enrich their non-work parts of life.

An attorney nearing his 40th birthday contacted my psychologist husband for personal counseling. He had reached tremendous career and financial success and approached this professional mentor to help him reach some emotional and spiritual goals.

We psychologists and other trained helpers now see such seekers every day. I'm excited to see how people are re-evaluating what's important.

This could be your reason for reading this book. If so, you'll see how to develop mentoring relationships for all parts of your life.

4. The new mentors have new, more stringent expectations.

In the 1980s and 1990s, many mentors were caught unaware by the fresh stampede of eager would-be proteges. More than a few top-level mentors told me they suffered mentor burnout from being approached so often and agreeing to do too much for their proteges. Several told me they'd never take on the role again.

Fortunately, the new mentors are setting a few boundaries for themselves. They say no to unreasonable demands. Even more so than in the past, people who would make great mentors are extremely busy and stretched very thin. As a result of their tight schedules and the steady demands on their time, these mentors now expect more preparation and follow through from their proteges.

For example, a senior manager I'll call Marnie was selected to be a mentor in one of Hewlett-Packard Company's mentoring programs. In order to maximize time and effects, Marnie asks her mentee to plan agendas and bring specific, thought-out questions and situations she faces to their meetings. They take time to make small talk, laugh, and share personal adventures, but they zero in on the mentee's learning and other goals sooner than their predecessors probably would have.

Many of their sessions are on the phone, and Marnie often sends suggestions to her mentee by e-mail and fax. When she can't provide something for her mentee, she tells her no without guilt, although she always tries to suggest an alternative.

The new mentees are discovering they have to keep commitments—or they'll be dropped in favor of replacements who will. This is a new trend that is likely to continue through this decade.

5. The new mentors and proteges don't cling to age traditions.

In the past, mentors tended to be at least a decade older than their mentees. Today, older mentors still exist and continue to be as helpful as ever. Certain kinds of experience and influence require decades to attain.

However, increasing numbers of young, successful individuals—particularly women and minority group members—are proving that they also have what it takes to be effective mentors. They know that a mentor's influence and experience count more than age. They like this new mentor role and aren't threatened by the wave of newcomers nipping at their heels.

At the same time, mentees are ignoring age barriers for themselves. In the past, proteges were always young, at least much younger than their mentors. After a certain age, it was considered too late or at least strange to benefit from a mentor's assistance. Now, those unwritten rules have changed. Older individuals are having to retrench in changed settings, and they want to quickly learn the ropes. That includes finding younger mentors with experience and wisdom that the older mentees need.

6. The new mentors and proteges are women and minorities.

As you probably know by now, the U.S. and Canadian work force is dramatically changing. By 2010, most new workers will be females and members of minority groups instead of Caucasian males.[1] Organizations see the value of preparing women and minorities as well as majority males through mentoring and other strategies to be managers of diverse employees and inclusive organizational cultures.

Cross-gender and cross-racial mentoring is common. Sam, a southern Caucasian prison warden trained in mentoring skills by the state corrections system, found himself mentoring Richard, an African-American participant in the agency's fast-track management development program. Neither was totally comfortable in his role, but they plugged away, talking about their feelings and their sometimes differing world views at each step of their relationship.

Howard, a Caucasian high-tech company president, interviewed three finalists in the company's formal mentoring program and chose to mentor Maria, an Hispanic manager in the finance department. Maria, who also interviewed three prospective mentors, ranked Howard her first choice. She expressed excitement, not at being linked with the company president, but at being able to share information about finance with a marketing expert.

Richard, Maria, and females and minority group members like them will soon be the mentors of the next generation of young employees.

Thanks to General Colin Powell (Ret.) and his staff at America's Promise,[2] mentoring is a household word in the homes of millions of American youth and their mentors. Thousands of excellent programs now teach kids of every background how to work with mentors and adults how to provide "cross-difference" mentoring[3] that genuinely improves lives.

7. The new relationships are short term and focus on skills and practical issues.

When I conducted my original research on mentoring in the 1970s,[4] I was fascinated to hear and read the tales of individuals who enjoyed long, productive, sometimes stormy relationships with their mentors, relationships that occasionally lasted for decades. Times were changing, but there was still a very parent-child feel to many of the stories. Romances between mentors and proteges weren't uncommon.

During the past 23 years, the typical length and focus of mentoring relationships took noticeable turns. Mentors and mentees are now very pragmatic. Even informal mentoring relationships are more structured than they used to be. Mentees typically identify one to three *skills* or *competencies* to develop with their mentors' help.

Prospective mentors and mentees know better than their predecessors how and what to negotiate. They set expectations, talk about rules, outline measurable goals, and agree on a relatively short time frame for the relationships.

You, too, can find these short-term goal-focused relationships very powerful. You may want to nurture an occasional long-term mentoring connection; but today's world favors short-term mentoring commitments and immediate results.

8. The new mentors and proteges are embracing formalized mentoring.

Two decades ago, mentoring was starting to be used as a deliberate corporate strategy to develop employees. Enthusiastic human resource managers began to design formal mentoring programs in an effort to help everyone get mentored. Several programs succeeded and are still going strong today.

But many leaders shook their heads in frustration because their efforts fizzled. The cry went up: "You can't force mentoring! It has to happen naturally or not at all."

Many professionals started to get gunshy about planned mentoring efforts. Anything except spontaneous, informal mentoring became controversial.

Fortunately, research on formalized or planned mentoring has been plentiful over the past few decades. Such experts as Kathy Kram, Bill and Marilynne Gray, Elizabeth Alleman, Margo Murray, Suzanne Karl, Jim Clawson, Michael Zey, Gail Holmes and her staff at Menttium, those of us at The Mentoring Group, and others have examined theories and applications in hundreds of settings and thousands of relationships.

The results? *Planned mentoring has been improved and is now an acceptable strategy in organizations of every kind.* The new mentors and proteges are willingly participating in these orchestrated opportunities. As you'll see in Chapter 12, you and your organization now have numerous choices about the amount and types of interventions to use.

These, then, are the new mentors and proteges. One characteristic they have in common is their desire to master the basics. To be sure you know the nuts and bolts, go on to Chapter 2. You'll learn some myths and truths that should take some bumps out of your mentoring journey.

2

The Truth about Mentors

WANTED IMMEDIATELY: Successful, powerful mentor to take willing protege under his/her wing, teach ropes, open doors, provide unfailing encouragement. Fee generous.

I thought about running that ad one time. I was feeling unsuccessful, unappreciated, and just about at the end of my rope professionally as well as personally. I had the right training and credentials, plenty of energy, and good intentions, but I was stuck. And I was too stubborn to ask anyone for help.

Fortunately for me, I fell into a relationship with an incredible mentor who stood me on my feet, taught me what I was doing wrong, and showed me what to do next.

A miracle? Maybe. Certainly it was a miracle that the relationship went so well, considering what I didn't know at the time about mentors and proteges and how they can affect each other. But now I *do* know what went on in that relationship—what I did to attract that mentor, what he got out of the exchange, what worked, and what didn't work for us.

Since then I've become intrigued with the concept of mentoring and have been involved with thousands of mentoring relationships. The conclusion: *Finding and making use of the right mentors is the most critical step you'll ever take in your career.*

And that's true no matter what career you're pursuing. I'm also convinced that you can learn to be an extremely effective mentor, one who makes significant, positive differences in the lives of others.

Mentoring is a strategy that successful people have known about for centuries. Almost all of them have had at least one significant mentor who helped them in some dramatic way.

David Packard and Bill Hewlett, founders of Hewlett-Packard Company, one of the stellar global corporations, were strongly influenced early in their careers by Stanford professor Fred Terman. In Packard's words, "It was Fred who sparked my interest in

electronics and who later encouraged and
helped Bill Hewlett and me go into business
for ourselves. His interest and faith in our
abilities, even at our young age and in the
midst of the Great Depression, *gave us confidence and helped set a course for us"* (em-
phasis added).[1]

Jane Evans rocketed to the top of I.
Miller Shoes at 25, thanks to a lot of ability
and the help of Maxie Jarmon, the chairman
of the board of I. Miller's parent corporation,
Genesco. She told me, "Jarmon was well
known for recognizing talent in women and
feeling that women should be put in positions of management. . . . He was really
there to prod my career for the first couple
of years. That was very important to me,
knowing that the chairman of the board was
interested in my progress."[2]

When Margaret Mead studied at Columbia University, she decided she wanted to
be a student of anthropologist Franz Boas.
Through him she could become part of a
handful of scholars in a field that was just
starting to gain acceptance and prestige in
America. In *Blackberry Winter*, she notes
that her initial strategy was to nod thought-
fully every time Boas made a point in class.
Boas noticed and went out of his way to give
Mead special attention. Her legendary career was launched.[3]

A young Italian painter apprenticed
himself to an older artist for six years and

then graduated to become a full-fledged assistant. Five years later, when the painter became prominent, he took on an apprentice of his own, passing his knowledge on to the next new talent. The painter's name was Leonardo de Vinci, and his teacher was Andrea del Verrocchio.[4]

Would these individuals have made it without their mentors? Maybe. But they didn't wait around to find out. Each of them took specific action to engage in mentoring, which dramatically changed his or her life forever.

You're starting to learn many of these techniques and strategies, why some mentoring relationships work and why others don't get off the ground in the first place—or else end badly for one or both members of the pair. Let's take a look at some of the common myths you may have learned to believe.

Mentoring Myths

Many people are confused about mentors and a little awed by the phenomenon of mentoring. They have misconceptions about how it works. To see what your current understanding of mentors and the mentoring process is, take a moment to answer true or false to the following statements.

True False

___ ___   1. Mentors are going out of style.

___ ___   2. Mentors should be older than their proteges.

___ ___   3. Mentoring relationships should be close and last at least a year.

___ ___   4. Mentors do the choosing, and it's best to wait for one to approach you.

___ ___   5. All mentoring relationships are different. You can't predict or control what happens.

___ ___   6. The relationship only benefits the protege.

___ ___   7. A person shouldn't have more than one mentor at a time.

___ ___   8. Male-female mentoring relationships generally end up as romances.

___ ___   9. Good mentoring relationships won't run into difficulties.

___ ___   10. Mentors are the easy way to
                 get ahead.

The answer to every one of these statements is false!

1. Mentors are definitely *not* going out of
style. In fact, their use is increasing. True,
the rules have changed, and their functions
generally differ from those in da Vinci's day,
but they're still the most powerful and practical help you can have to reach your goals.
You still need ability to make it, but you
need human helpers, too.

2. Mentors are generally older than their
mentees, but many are either the same age
or even younger. *The key is that the mentor
has skills, knowledge, or power you need but
don't have.*

3. Mentoring relationships don't have to be
particularly close, and their lengths vary.
Some relationships are quite formal, and one
or both people maintain emotional distance.
Lengths range all the way from a few significant encounters to years.

4. Mentors can initiate the relationship,
but you shouldn't wait for a mentor to approach you. You can do many things to make
yourself competitive in what continues to be

a "mentors' market." You can approach the people you'd like to help you.

5. Mentoring relationships have definite, predictable patterns and cycles. By knowing what to expect, you can influence what happens to you.

6. The relationship benefits both partners. Although the mentee should gain the most, the mentor benefits significantly. Once you know what your mentors are getting out of your relationships, you'll probably shed any guilt you have about being on the receiving end.

7. Not only is it possible to have more than one mentor at a time, you should. But acquire your multiple mentors with care.

8. Male-female mentoring relationships do *not* have to end up in a romance. In fact, this step is very risky.

9. All mentoring relationships run into some challenges. The key is learning how to handle them. Your relationships can actually benefit from these tough, growth-producing times.

10. Using mentors isn't necessarily the easy way of getting ahead. Finding the right mentors takes effort on your part. It in-

volves extra work, the stretching of your limits, and new commitments and risks. Mentors can be demanding, and they can have inappropriate expectations of you. Although they may have the best of intentions, they can try to steer you toward their own goals instead of yours.

I'd like to shatter the mentoring myths once and for all, so that you can make mentoring work for you. Your potential mentors at this point may know more about their careers and some aspects of success than you do, but you're going to know more about mentoring than they do. This insight is going to enable you to initiate and enjoy at least one successful mentoring relationship. Not only that, your experiences are going to be exciting!

Mentors Defined

The word *mentor* has its origins thousands of years ago in Greek mythology in the tale of Odysseus. When Odysseus set out for the Trojan War, he entrusted his son, Telemachus, to his friend and advisor, Mentor. While Odysseus was gone, Mentor served as guardian, teacher, and father figure to his young protege. Occasionally, Athena, goddess of wisdom and the arts, would disguise herself as Mentor and appear in his stead.

Today, mentors are *experienced people who go out of their ways to: (1) help you clarify your vision and personal goals and (2) build skills to reach them.* They have power—through whom and what they know—to help you succeed.

Most publications and organizations use the word mentor to describe the helper, but many others favor the term coach. In my opinion, a mentor *can* be a coach, that is, teach and give you feedback on specific skills. At the same time, a good mentor provides *more* than that. He or she is someone who helps you step out of your everyday box, look at the grand picture of your life, and work on goals that are vital to you.

A mentor might *not* be an expert on the particular skill you're developing, but he or she can be your *learning broker*, accountability partner, cheerleader, and sounding board to help you find all the help you need to master that skill and more.

Mentors can have a dramatic and intense impact on your life, and often they can help engineer critical turning points. If your relationship is a "primary" one, there's probably a very personal and emotional bond between the two of you. This emotional attachment, particularly on your part, is due to your realization that your mentor is going considerably out of his or her way to help you—taking risks, going out on a limb, and showing what seems like a prejudiced interest in your behalf.

In the mid-1970s, psychologist and Yale professor Daniel Levinson described this primary-type mentor in the lives of males he was studying at the time: ". . . The mentor takes the younger man under his wing, invites him into a new occupational world, shows him around, imparts his wisdom, cares, sponsors, criticizes, and bestows his blessing. The teaching and the sponsoring have their values, but the blessing is the crucial element."[5]

Today we recognize the value of primary mentors and also see the major value of less intense yet extremely helpful "secondary" mentors. These are people who enter your life at important transitions, times when you need to learn quickly. The relationships can be short and businesslike, and yet you can gain a great deal from them.

Your best approach is to concentrate on acquiring multiple secondary mentors. You can acquire them all at one time or one after the other, if that sounds more manageable.

Proteges by Any Other Name . . .

The word *protege* comes from the French verb, *proteger*, to protect, and it's used here to denote both men and women who are helped to reach their career and life goals by mentors. You'll sometimes see diacritical marks on the word (protégé), but I choose not to use them. The term has been largely replaced by mentee, although several publications and organizations still use protege. Others prefer terms such as mentoree, associate, trainee, partner, aspirant, learner, or participant.

Now that you're familiar with the definitions and have a glimpse of the truth about mentors, you're well on your journey. Whether you're a mentor or a mentee—and you're likely to play both roles with different people—you'll be affected by the same ingredients and dynamics that have touched people from Gloria Estefan to Michelangelo, Aristotle to Margaret Mead, Colin Powell to Kathleen Kennedy Townsend to Bill Walsh.

If you're a bright, ambitious achiever who's heard about mentoring but don't know how to do it, you've found your answer. If you're a recent graduate stymied by what to do with the next phase of your life, you'll see how to use mentoring to help. If you're ready to change your career but are overwhelmed by the changes facing you, you'll see how the right mentors can help you around the obstacles you fear.

Your journey continues in the next chapter, as we look closely at the splendid advantages that mentors provide.

3

The Mentor Advantages

All men have the stars ... but they are
not the same things for different people.
For some ... the stars are guides. For
others they are no more than lights in
the sky ....
　　　　　　—Antoine de St. Exupery
　　　　　　THE LITTLE PRINCE

Good mentors give their proteges what they need. For Bill Hewlett and David Packard, good mentoring meant inspiration and direction from their professor. For Margaret Mead, it was a ticket to a South Sea island. In my case, it meant a good push at the right time to get me moving again.

A Look at Your Past "Mentors"

One of the best ways for you to affect your mentoring future is to learn from your life up to now. I'd like to bring back some faded memories from your past. Get very comfortable, and start to think about the people significant to you, your career, and your life in general. You may never have called these people "mentors" before.

Sit back and picture the various stages of your life, starting with when you were a young child. What adults were important to you? Who made a difference in your young life?

Picture your teen years. Whose face comes into your mind? Your young adult years?

Make a list of these important people.

Now picture all of these mentors together in one room. They're sitting around a large conference table, and you're the topic of conversation.

What are all these important people saying about you? How do their perceptions differ? Who's sitting at the head of the table, chairing the meeting? Which ones have only a few comments to offer? Are some people surprised to be included with your other mentors? Take some time to compile a complete list.

What feelings do these people still evoke in you? Pride? Gratitude? Amusement? Admiration? Sadness? Frustration?

Were some *primary* mentoring relationships, ones that carried strong emotions for one or both of you? Were several *secondary* mentors, people who provided important help at key times? What kind of pattern is developing as you grow older? If you're typical, you had more helpers when you were younger.

Although they all provided mentoring for you in the broad sense, each form of help was slightly different, depending on what you wanted or needed at the time and what those helpers were able to give you. Some of what you got from them probably came about because you were clever enough to take it without your mentors even knowing it.

Next to each name, write at least *one specific thing* each person did for or gave to you. Keep this help in mind as we examine the most common types of advantages that mentors give their mentees.

Help with Your Goals

One of the first things mentors can do for you is help you set or clarify some specific goals for yourself. In fact, mentors usually love to take on the role of advisor and sounding board, and in that role they'll pass on great quantities of advice to you, probably more than you ask for.

When you find mentors who aren't only good advice-givers but good listeners who tune into what you're really saying and help you identify the goals you want, you've hit the jackpot.

A landscape designer I'll call Jack described how he played counselor with Sam, his strapping 20-year-old assistant. At least once a week the two of them went out for a pitcher of beer and evening of heart-to-heart talk. "Sam will talk to me about almost everything—his career, girlfriends or lack of them, family, whatever. I think he just likes me to listen, although every once in a while I throw in some advice."

When I talked to Sam, I learned that he was getting much more out of their conversations than his mentor thought. "What I think Jack is doing for me is more or less tracing a path. Before I met him, I knew what I had to offer, but I didn't know how to use it. He's helping me figure out what I have to do, step by step, not just about my job, although he helps a lot with that, but about my whole life."

Kathryn, a bank manager, asked her assistant and mentee Jackie to prepare some six-month, one-year, and five-year career goals for herself. Jackie told me, "I thought that was a great idea. Well, it was fairly easy writing the six-month goals, and even the one-year ones weren't bad. But I had a terrible time with the five-year goals. I wasn't absolutely sure I wanted to stay in banking. My husband Mario and the kids were still the most important thing in my life, and I was a little afraid to tell Kathryn that.

"When I finally brought it up with Kathryn, she was great. She helped me think about some life goals, besides those for my career, like what I wanted in terms of my family relationships, my spiritual needs, my health, and so on."

You'll gain a great advantage if you find a mentor to help you clarify—then reach—the goals you're passionate about.

Encouragement

Encouragement is the fuel that all of us need to excel. In *Encouraging the Heart*, leadership and management experts, James M. Kouzes and Barry Z. Posner, provide strong evidence of the power of encouragement to motivate and change people's lives for the better.[1]

According to my own research, encouragement is the mentor advantage that successful people mention most often. *They say it's the help they value most from their mentors.* Their best mentors encouraged them to be all they could be, with an almost prejudiced, unfailing confidence in them.

This unflagging faith boosted their self-esteem in a way that mere advice or a pat on the head never could.

Jackie described how Kathryn's encouragement helped her turn the corner. Despite her joy at being selected for her bank's fast-track management training program, Jackie felt uneasy about her ability to handle it. Could she really do the work? Would this affect her relationship with her family? Could she really live up to the expectations of her mentor?

Over a relaxed dinner, Kathryn told Jackie what happened to her when she was selected for the same program five years before. "I was the only woman in a class of 12. What's worse, all the men except two had MBAs. I only had a bachelor's, like you, but mine was in English! I knew I was only there because of the pressure being put on the bank to promote women, and I was scared to death at the first training session.

"You can imagine how enthusiastic I felt when the male instructor looked at me and said, 'Well, it looks like they've sent one of the secretaries to take notes today.' That's just how I felt, too. Like a little girl with her note pad and pen in there with all the big boys. Jackie, if I could do it, so can you. Besides, you have 10 years' knowledge about the bank behind you plus a degree in business. You also have me, and I won't let you down."

"I really needed to hear that," Jackie confessed. "She took a genuine interest in me, and she was the only one who did at the time. Even my husband told me I'd never make it. Kathryn encouraged me to try new things and to make my own decisions, right or wrong. Somehow I walked into that training program on the first day and survived. I did well, in fact."

Has there already been someone in your life who conveyed a strong faith in your abilities? Perhaps more faith than you had? Did this expressed confidence in you motivate you to prove that you really could accomplish what that person expected?

More than 30 years ago, Harvard researchers Robert Rosenthal and Lenore Jacobson conducted a classic series of experiments.[2] Teachers were told by the research team that several of their students had scored as "intellectual bloomers" on intelligence tests, when in reality these students had received scores similar to the control group.

At the end of the school year, during which the "bloomers" were also informed of their status, the researchers asked these teachers to complete ability ratings on all the students in their classes. The teachers identified the so-called "bloomers" as superior. Indeed, their performances *were* better than the others, even than those students who actually scored in the high range on the IQ tests.

This fascinating phenomenon is called the Self-Fulfilling Prophecy or the Pygmalion Effect.

Experts offer many explanations for this phenomenon. Some say that if you put a label on someone, you'll actually start *acting differently* toward that person.

Thinking that the average students were gifted, the teachers probably spent more time with them and were more earnestly complimentary about their work in anticipation of greater achievements. Since these students received so much attention, they naturally accomplished more than their peers did.

A parallel theory says that when given a label for themselves, people will start responding in ways that they think characterize people with that label. When the "intellectual bloomers" learned of their status, they probably worked harder than they ever had since they knew that "good" students always applied themselves. And since they worked harder, their performance naturally improved.

This complex interaction happens in many mentoring relationships. A mentor who believes you have great potential can inspire you to believe in yourself and thus cause you to try harder.

In commenting about her mentor, one protege described this process. "He liked what I did and would challenge me as though I were an equal. He gave me just enough of the needle to spur me on without giving me so much that I became embittered or discouraged. He'd always urge me to take on things I thought I couldn't do, and he was right. I would say that good mentoring is encouragement and support. It's the recognition that you're a human being and your IQ is at least as high as anybody else's."

Think about the kinds of encouragement that motivate you. It might be regular doses of praise given directly to you, compliments made about you in front of others, an occasional pat on the back, or a tangible reward such as a present, a raise, a better job title, or a few days off.

The right mentor can and should give you the kind of encouragement you need, although *you'll possibly have to teach him or her how to do it*. More about that later.

New or Improved Skills and Knowledge

A glance at history reveals countless examples of masters teaching their crafts to young apprentices. The apprentice, usually a boy, generally left his home and went to live with a master carpenter, silversmith, artist, shoemaker, or musician. For several years, the master diligently tutored the young apprentice until he was ready to "graduate" and earn his own way. Later on, the new craftsman passed on these skills to apprentices of his own.

This concept continues in essence today in apprenticeship programs, teacher training, student internships in business and government, and resident and intern training for physicians. In each of these programs, skills and knowledge are formally and informally passed on to the "apprentice" students.

Most mentors instruct as a key part of their role. A former mentee talked about the best mentor he ever had. "Sometimes he told me what something meant or how to do it. Other times he demonstrated what to him was the right way and then asked me to do it while he watched. Often he'd criticize what I'd done, sometimes kindly and patiently, other times so harshly that I had to bite the side of my cheek to keep from crying. Whatever he did, I learned from that man. He was a great teacher."

Mentors are usually chosen because they have knowledge and skills that proteges want. Teaching and coaching are what most mentors do. Sometimes this instructing is formal, but it's usually more of a tutoring and coaching process.

Jean Charcot, a successful French neurologist, was Sigmund Freud's teacher in

Paris for only four and a half months, but he had an irrevocable and powerful impact upon his protege's life. According to Freud's biographer, "It would be hard to overestimate Freud's lasting identification with Charcot." Freud kept a photo of Charcot on his wall and said later, "No one has ever affected me in the same way."[3]

Charcot taught Freud how to trust and defend the purely clinical evidence that he collected on his patients' psychoses, even when it didn't coincide with the prevailing theories of the time. Freud sharpened his observational skills as he learned ". . . to follow the unforgotten advice of my master, Charcot: to look at the same things again and again until they themselves begin to speak."

When good mentors realize that they alone can't provide you with all the skills and knowledge you need, they essentially play the role of *learning broker*. They'll refer you to other people, classes, books, or additional resources to help you learn.

I interviewed several of the women named by *Business Week* magazine as the 100 top corporate women in America.[4] Many of them had outstanding bosses who taught them everything they could and then sent them off for more training.

For example, a vice-president said, "My mentor told me that I had to continue my education. He insisted that I go to law school at night so that I could move ahead in a law firm and then a corporation without being affected by discrimination against women."

A company president had a similar experience at the beginning of her career. "He put me through every sales, advertising, and marketing course available in New York City. During the years I worked for him, I went to school four nights a week."

Former Forty-Niners football coach Bill Walsh received valuable teaching from at least one of his mentors, Paul Brown, then with the Cincinnati Bengals. Brown hired Walsh and gave him straight-forward advice that greatly influenced his coaching style and philosophy with mentees of his own.[5] Walsh, in turn, went on to provide what I'd call mentoring for an amazing number of successful National Football League coaches.[6]

Do you have to learn how to tackle a major project? Do you want to know how to balance work and the rest of your life? How to negotiate contracts? The best ways to get published? The right mentors are waiting to teach you how to do it.

Models to Follow

It's always interesting to watch how other people handle situations that have baffled us or that may be looming in our futures. What fascinates us is exactly how they do it and what happens to them as a result of their actions. Depending on the results, we may copy their behavior, reject it, or come up with a compromise that blends their method with our own. Stanford professor Albert Bandura has done extensive research on these principles, incorporating them into his Self-Efficacy Theory.[7]

Mentors can purposely provide that modeling for you—or model without realizing it—while you listen and watch. One of my most important mentors, Warren Schmidt, was a powerful role model for me during my graduate school work. All of us students watched and listened to everything he did and tried to copy it. I'm sure he had no idea we did this. To this day, I still ask myself before moving ahead, "What would Warren do?"

In *They Call Me Coach*, former UCLA basketball coach John Wooden gives credit for much of his coaching style to his former coach Ward "Piggy" Lambert of Purdue. "Players had tremendous respect for him. He worked hard and expected you to work hard. It is because of his theory [on players needing to be in condition] that I have based my entire coaching career on a similar thesis."[8]

Fashion supermodel and entrepreneur Cheryl Tiegs said that her mentors were magazine editor Julie Brett and agents Bar-

bara Stone and Nina Blanchard. Tiegs
watched these women closely and imitated a
lot of what she saw. Tiegs went on to become a mentor herself and served a stint as
chairperson of Clairol's National Mentor
Program.[9]

In *The Person Who Changed My Life*,
Kathleen Kennedy Townsend describes one
of her strongest role models, University of
New Mexico law professor Ruth Kovnat.
"Ruth showed me how a woman could fulfill
her potential in the professional world while
also being a wonderful wife and mother. This
was extremely rare in the early 1970s, when
the lack of role models forced many women
into the false choice of either one or the
other."[10]

Role models who are like you aren't
always easy to find, especially if you're a
woman, a member of a minority group, or
anyone trying to break a new gender, racial,
or age barrier. Just such a mentor paved the
way for Grace, a dynamic young African-
American woman who's a lawyer for a record
company. Grace had nothing but praise for
her mentor and immediate boss, one of the
senior attorneys in the company.

"She's the perfect role model—smart,
dedicated, funny, respected by everyone.
She works hard but knows how to play and
relax, too. She has given me insight in how
to handle racist and sexist men and women,
too, for that matter. I see how her rules of

personal behavior keep her ethically way above those around her. It really helps me to have her around as a kind of mirror."

A number of mentees praise mentors who were extremely demanding of them. They didn't particularly enjoy the periods of struggle they underwent at the hands of their mentors, and they didn't adopt all the techniques they witnessed, but they respected their former mentors for sticking to their principles. They also radiate a certain pride for surviving these sometimes grueling tests.

Former U.S. President Jimmy Carter recalls what it was like to work for his former boss, Admiral Hyman Rickover. "He may not have cared or known it, certainly not at that time, but Admiral Rickover had a profound effect on my life, perhaps more than anyone except my own parents. He was unbelievably hard working and competent, and he demanded total dedication from his subordinates. We feared and respected him and strove to please him."[11]

Mentors aren't always aware of their impact. Eva, a retired school principal was always immensely popular with her faculty and students but was genuinely surprised to discover just how much influence she had on many of the members of her staff.

"They never said anything about it when we worked together, but when I ran into them later, they said they watched and copied everything I did. They told me about dozens of incidents in which they asked each other, 'What would Eva do now?' They said that my influence even spilled over to their private lives. I was absolutely floored."

Over time, a mentor demonstrates a certain standard of conduct and success. He or she presents one version of excellence: *You decide whether or not it fits your values—and whether or not it's worth imitating.*

Opportunities to Perform

Sometimes all you need is a chance to show what you can do, and mentors can give you that break. Once Michelangelo had completed his training, the powerful Medici family of Florence saw that he had the space, money, and contacts he needed to continue his extraordinary career.

For 10 years, Breuer not only influenced Freud and challenged him on an intellectual level, but he loaned money and referred patients to him so that Freud could concentrate on his work instead of finances.

All during drama school at Yale and afterward, entertainer Dick Cavett spent a lot of energy figuring out ingenious ways to meet celebrities.[12] His strategies usually worked, much to the amazement of his friends. His dream was to make it in show business, so he answered casting calls in

New York City, continued to meet stars, and
constantly watched for his chance.

While working for *Time* magazine as a
copy boy, he read that Jack Paar was always looking for material for his opening
monologue for the "Tonight Show." Cavett
wrote a few pages of how he thought a Paar
monologue should sound, put them into an
official *Time* envelope, and then "acciden-
tally" met Paar in a corridor of the RCA
building.

After getting Paar's attention (he said
that *Time* was considering doing a story on
him, which wasn't true), Cavett offered Paar
the jokes. That same night, Paar slipped a
few of the lines into the monologue and got
some laughs. Cavett again "bumped into"
Paar, who suggested that Cavett write a few
more. Cavett leaped at the chance and a
week later was hired as a talent coordinator
and sometime writer for the show. Cavett
had the skills and chutzpah, and Paar gave
him his first big break.

Ideally, when you're ready to make
your debut, it will be in a safe setting where
you won't make any drastic mistakes. A
good mentor will recognize when you're ready
to take that step, maybe even before you
make that recognition.

One woman told me, "The best thing he
did for me as a mentor was to let me try my
wings in the company. I was the only female
there, by the way, but there was never any

problem about my being a woman. He let me try some of my own far-fetched ideas, like the time I invited the L.A. Dodgers to our board meeting. He also nudged me a little now and then to try something I was a little afraid to do. But I don't think he ever let me go further out on a limb than I could handle."

Good mentors will tread that delicate line between telling you what to do and providing you with enough freedom to explore and test new waters on your own. As your skills, determination, and courage grow, your mentor should pull back, allow you a little more freedom, provide more opportunities for you, and let you go your own way. Sometimes this is easier said than done.

When Mead finished her course work in anthropology and was ready to do her fieldwork for her thesis, she had her heart set on going to Polynesia but needed a fellowship to pay the way. Boas, her professor, was afraid that a young woman like Mead wouldn't be able to handle the rigors of life in the remote islands, so he insisted that she study American Indians instead. Mead was determined to go to Polynesia, however, and made up her mind to convince Boas to let her have her way.

The two argued for quite a while, and after some fervent selling on Mead's part and her not-so-subtle hinting that Boas was unliberated, undemocratic, and somewhat of a bully, he finally gave in. Once he did, however, he backed her completely and made sure she got her fellowship.

Good athletic coaches find themselves playing this kind of mentoring role nearly every day of their lives. Wooden was a master at knowing just what help to give each of his players. Although his whole approach stressed the needs of the team over the individual players, he always looked out for the special things his players needed, no matter how small.

For example, for Bill Walton, it was making it as easy as possible for him to play basketball with his bad knees. This meant allowing him to call a time-out whenever he felt the need for one and letting him decide himself if he would practice on the Monday following a game.

Some of the resources and opportunities that mentors provide will focus on the specific career moves you should make. They might hire you themselves, as Paar hired Cavett; they might get you raises and promotions. They could take you along with them when they transfer to new jobs or help you transfer by yourself. They might even fire you.

Kathryn helped Jackie write and rewrite her resume and suggested how to fill out the application forms for the bank's management training program. She wrote a strong letter of recommendation for Jackie, talked with the selection committee, and later covered for her on the job so that Jackie could concentrate on her training and still keep a home life.

Money, a job, physical space, a stage and a spotlight, a ticket to the South Seas. Whatever you need to facilitate that break, mentors can help you get it.

Increased Visibility

Once good mentors are convinced that you have what it takes to be a success, they'll go out of their ways to be sure that you're seen and heard by those in positions to help you. They'll make it a point to introduce you around, include you in important meetings and conferences, make sure that you're noticed at those meetings, and share some of their spotlights with you.

Mildred, a corporate executive, blushed as she recalled the unexpected visibility she received as a beginning salesclerk and the new protege of an influential sales manager. Her mentor had just finished giving the entire sales force a rousing pep talk on how he wanted this Christmas season to break all records.

"Suddenly he started talking about me. He told them what I had accomplished over the previous six months and told them to do exactly what I did. He even said I could sell the fixtures right off the floor! I really couldn't have at that point, but when he said that I made up my mind that I'd work my tail off trying! I was offered several new opportunities as a result of that incident."

Similarly, Kathryn described how she helped Jackie become more visible. "I made sure that she got on the committee for the bank's Christmas party for refugees, one of the president's favorite causes. He mentioned to me later that he was impressed with the way she got things done.

"When she was still my secretary, I had the rules changed so she could travel with me on business trips, something only the secretaries of the very top officers of the bank had been allowed to do. After a while I sent her on trips alone, and she did beautifully."

Another mentor provided her protege, Max, with visibility by asking him to write a chapter in her book and making sure that his name appeared as the chapter's author. This was especially helpful to Max because he wanted to teach in college and needed to have several publications on his resume. The chapter turned out well, and Max was even able to publish a slightly different version of it in a major journal. His mentor had nothing to lose (she, in fact, saved herself considerable writing time), and Max had everything to gain from this gesture.

The visibility you get, provided it makes you look good, will have a direct impact on how well you're accepted in your career field. Although we'd like to think that merely doing an excellent job is a guarantee of recognition, that assumption is naive.

Your ideas are much more likely to be accepted and noticed if they're promoted or even casually mentioned by someone important. The person who sponsors you will at least partially determine who ultimately listens to your ideas.

As an additional bonus for you, these signs of recognition will probably increase your motivation and reinforce your commitment. They'll also intensify your feelings of professional identity. And the fact that an important or respected person is willing to tell the rest of the world that he or she has checked you out, found you acceptable, and is willing to be responsible for you only reinforces this sense of identity.

If for some reason you don't perform well, your mentors can share the blame!

A Bridge to Maturity

We all have to experience what social psychologists call "anticipatory socialization" in order to be successful as adults in our careers and in the other parts of our lives. This means that in order to perform well in your role as an adult, you have to first understand what that role involves—

and then you have to have the personal resources and skills you need to perform it. Mentors can initiate you into this process. Their guidance and example can be a bridge over the difficult transitions in your life. That tender, painful leap from youth to adulthood is rarely accomplished successfully without it. "I think of good mentoring as analogous to good parenting," Levinson told me. "Just as a parent brings a child into the world as a child, the mentor is a key figure in bringing a young adult into the world of adults and fostering development so that one can build a life that is meaningful."

In my opinion, good mentoring is more like good grandparenting. Parents have to be strict at times, discipline, and make their children eat their vegetables and go to bed on time. Grandparents (and mentors) are freer to inspire big dreams, encourage mentees to take risks, and let them eat chocolate pudding and watch videos until midnight if they want.

You've seen many of the specific advantages mentors can provide for you. The likes of Jimmy Carter, Bill Walton, Cheryl Tiegs, Sigmund Freud, Dick Cavett, Geraldine Ferraro, Michelangelo, Sandra Day O'Connor, Thomas Wolfe, and thousands of other successful people have enjoyed some or all of these mentor gifts. So can you.

4

It's a Two-Way Exchange

I benefit myself in aiding him.

—Sophocles

You may be thinking by this time that mentees gain an extraordinary amount from mentoring relationships. They do, but rest assured that mentoring is a *two-way exchange*, and your mentors also benefit enormously from your relationships, sometimes more than you do.

Your mentors have their own reasons for assisting you. They may be helping you because you have something they want or something they'll need in the future. Maybe they're attracted to you on a personal level.

Or you're assigned to them. Maybe you remind them of themselves at your age or someone they once knew and weren't able to help at the time. They could just have an intuitive feeling that they should help you.

Their reasons stem from a variety of sources, including their past experiences in similar relationships, their self-images, and their basic values, goals, and needs. Their getting involved with you depends partly on their stages of adult development.

My case studies reveal the following underlying motivations.

They're Getting More Work Done with Your Help

The most obvious and often the initial reason your mentors become involved is that you can do some of their work for them. Many people take on mentees because they're swamped with work or bored with details and need a helper to tie up loose ends.

Max's professor had to finish the manuscript for her new textbook within nine months. The fact that Max was willing (actually honored, he said) to write one of the chapters cut her writing time by at least a month. It also meant that the chapter would be better, thanks to Max's research and excellent writing skills.

A psychologist told me about an interesting mentoring relationship in which she and her mentor helped each other advance their goals. She was a therapist at a counseling center where her mentor was the deputy director. For various reasons, he was unable to implement several of his ideas, and he knew he'd never be promoted to the recently vacated director's job.

As an alternate strategy, he convinced the young woman to apply for the post, and he lobbied hard for her appointment. She got the position, and as a result of her support, he's been able to begin several new projects and carry out many of his ideas. Thanks to the flexibility of his "protege-boss," he now designs his own work responsibilities and arranges his hours to suit his life style. Had he not helped the willing young psychologist, he might never have realized his own career goals.

A mentor who's a pioneer in a new field may take on one or more proteges in order to finish his or her life's work. Mead's mentor, Boas, was such a pioneer. Mead describes his sense of urgency. "In 1924, there were four graduate students in anthropology at Columbia and a mere handful in other universities. He had to plan—much as if he were a general with only a handful of troops available to save a whole country—where to place each student most strategically so that each piece of work would count and nothing would be wasted and no piece of work would have to be done over." [1]

Freud was another pioneer who sought heirs to carry out his grand design. He consciously selected a number of followers, the most notable being Carl Gustav Jung, whom Freud called his "son and heir." Freud put great demands on Jung to continue the line of psychoanalytic discovery the former had started, and, for a while at least, Jung obliged his mentor.[2]

They're Grooming a Crucial Subordinate

Smart leaders have always known it's important to build a reliable team of colleagues and subordinates who will support and follow them. In the past, they were often reluctant to admit their weaknesses and surrounded themselves with subordinates who mirrored their strengths.

Although this leadership style still exists, modern leaders are more willing to acknowledge their flat sides, areas where they should be more well-rounded. To fill in these gaps, they choose and train subordinates who have abilities different from their own and who are willing to serve as their complements. For example, an expert in engineering seeks out an aide strong in finance.

Depending on your prospective mentor's approach, you might be eyed as a possible protege because you're very much like him or her. Conversely, you may be chosen because you have capabilities, contacts, or other advantages that your mentor lacks. "I needed an assistant I could count on," confided Kathryn. "I had to pull a staff together practically overnight. I didn't even have a secretary. Well, when Jackie was assigned to me, I was thrilled. I tend to be rather frantic and dash around a lot, so I saw in Jackie someone who could keep me on course, finish what I started."

Once you become crucial to your mentors, they'll probably depend on you for honest feedback, perhaps the only straight information they receive. Management consultant Eugene Jennings suggests that your mentors may depend on you to rescue them.[3] This could mean preventing them in advance from making costly mistakes, or it could mean helping them out of a dilemma by covering up their errors or taking the blame yourself.

Once you've been groomed, your mentor can feel free to move on without fear or guilt, confident that you can be either a suitable replacement or a valuable aide to take along. While governor of California, Jerry Brown appointed his longtime friend and campaign manager, Tom Quinn, as chair of the powerful California Air Resources Board. Quinn, in turn, hired a dynamic young lawyer, Mary Nichols, as one of his key assistants. When Quinn left the board to work on Brown's presidential campaign, he chose

Nichols as his replacement, knowing that he was leaving the job in good hands.

They're Being Rewarded for Developing Talent

When you perform well, you reflect favorably upon your mentors. This serves to validate your mentors' worth and good judgment, not only to themselves, but in the eyes of their bosses and peers.

Athletic coaches and managers are generously rewarded for locating and being effective with world-class players. College professors compete for top students and are admired and rewarded for grooming these stars. Sales managers woo the best sales reps from other companies and tangibly benefit from their finds.

Your past mentors received tangible or intangible rewards for developing you.

Of course, the reverse of this is also true. When you don't measure up, you reflect poorly on your mentors. In the novel, *Chimera*, the mentee Bellerophon pleads with his mentor, Polyeidus, not to give up on him. "Who remembers the helper if the hero doesn't make it?"[4] A writer made the same point about his former mentor. "He had to go out of his way for me because he didn't want me to fail. It would look bad for him."

They're Achieving Vicariously through You

Researchers suggest that some people need to achieve *directly*—for example, win a tennis tournament or get published—in order to be satisfied and personally fulfilled. But others don't need this direct kind of success, or at least not as much of it. These individuals are satisfied *vicariously*, through the achievements of people they know and influence.

Your mentors may feel fulfilled by associating and emotionally identifying with you as you achieve. Sometimes they get even more pleasure from watching and hearing about your successes than they do from their own.

There's another explanation for your mentors' vicarious achievement motivation. They may *prefer* to reach their goals directly but realize they never will. So they accept reality and concentrate instead on seeing that you make it. They may force themselves into accepting this vicarious style of achievement.

Think of the seasoned employee who, after 15 years in the same job, realizes that she's never going to become president of the company. This person has gone as far as possible and so takes it upon herself to befriend and coach all the new people, hoping that one or more of them will succeed and reach that pinnacle instead. Management expert Rosabeth Kanter calls such seasoned employees the "social professionals."[5]

Because they're somehow blocked from advancing completely up the ladder, they turn their energies elsewhere either outside the company to customers and colleagues, or downward to junior personnel.

An author shared his experience about his former mentor, a man with great goals. "I found out later from his wife, after he had died, that he was striving for a quality of excellence that he himself could never reach, never had reached. She said that was why he kept pressing me for that quality. When I published my first book, he was extremely proud. This is the kind of thing he would've liked to have done himself, but he just couldn't do it."

They're Investing in Your Future

A mentor who over the years helped several proteges made the following observation about her efforts. "Excuse the mixed metaphor, but the bread comes back buttered on the waters. Very often the people that you pass on turn up at another time in your life and are helpful to you in doing other things. I have found that all my life."

Individuals might serve as your mentors in order to gain a future return on their investments. Helping you is a way of storing a cache of owed favors from you that will pay off once you've succeeded and are out on your own. Many mentors build whole networks of proteges in various organizations and geographical locations. By cleverly increasing their contacts, they're able to reach more of their own goals.

"I had to laugh the first time I went into his office," said a former protege in reference to a well-known scholar. "It looked like the war room at the Pentagon. He had a map of the world on his office wall with little pins stuck all over it.

"Each pin was a former graduate student. Blue pins were the ones who were working for the government. Yellow ones were those teaching college. Red ones were in the business world. White ones were stuck out in the middle of the ocean because he'd lost track of what happened to them. I counted over 125 pins on that wall. It reminded me of Charlemagne and how he must have kept track of all his soldiers."

This mentor also had a card file of his graduates and kept in regular contact with them. He always turned to one of them first when he needed help writing an article or a research proposal, placing an upcoming graduate, or tracking down information. And they in turn always thought of him whenever they needed an outside consultant on one of their projects or advisory committees. His original investments paid off.

They're Repaying Past Debts

Hank's a very successful contractor in his late 30s. His business tripled in the last two years, making him a multi-millionaire. Hank confided that he was thrilled with his accomplishments but uneasy about his new success. His image as a high school dropout and rebel made him feel a little guilty. He felt that he hadn't really paid his dues, and no amount of reassurance from his friends or his wife was enough to assuage that guilt.

"When I get the tab at the end of this meal, I know how much it is, and I know where to pay it. But who do I pay for all this? I don't like having that enormous debt hanging over me."

I told him about the mentoring concept and about this book, both of which interested him tremendously. Although he'd always shunned help from anyone else, he became very interested in the possibility of mentoring others. It sounded to him like a good way of finally paying some dues.

About a year later I ran into Hank again. "Guess what?" he said with a big grin. "I hired two young guys in my office right after I saw you, and I'm teaching them the business. Both of them had gotten into a little trouble, so I convinced the judge to turn them over to me. I guess they reminded me a little of myself when I was their age. Well, it's working out just great, even though they're running me ragged. I also started teaching a contracting class at the community college."

Hank and mentors like him often take on mentees as an indirect way of paying their debts to society as a whole or to the specific people who once helped them. They believe that they were given a break at the right time and now are morally obligated to provide the same helping hand for others.

Laura, a satisfied architect, told me, "You have to pay your debts, for heaven's sake. When the opportunity comes, sometimes often, sometimes only once, don't miss it. You still owe it. We rarely have the opportunity to help those who helped us, so we help others."

They're Remedying the Situation for Underdogs

Some of the so-called underdogs of our society—women, racial and ethnic minorities, and persons with disabilities, to name a few—who succeed forget their climbs and do very little to help counterparts who follow them. But a larger number are committed to helping other underdogs face and resolve the social and economic hurdles in the way.

An African-American executive described how he tries to give young Blacks an extra push. "If I hear of an opportunity somewhere, or if we're going to have an opening on the staff, I'll say, 'Well, you've got to consider so and so' because I want a brother to have a shot at it. That doesn't always make me very popular around here, but I don't give a damn. If I don't practice what I preach about equal opportunities, I might as well go back to the ghetto."

A successful female fashion designer remarked, "I really had a struggle, even though this field is one of the few that has always been open to women. My family was poor, and every cent I made I had to turn over to them. When I finally got to where I wanted to be, I decided I'd do something for the people—women especially—who were trying to do similar things. I've sponsored at least 10 young women and have been called a female chauvinist as a result, but I don't even care."

Another woman explained why she does her mentoring, again mostly for women. "I try to help because women desperately need help in getting ahead. No one should ever go through what I had to go through. It's ridiculous, but we need a network of women to prevent that sort of thing. The amount of effort it took me to get from square A to square B was criminal."

Now that diversity is the goal and soon-to-be norm in business, former underdogs will have more chances to make key differences.

They're Enjoying a Positive Relationship

Many mentors, by the nature of their high-level or demanding positions, lack close friends. As a result, many of them naturally welcome the eager attention and admiration of good proteges. They crave that sense of being needed, depended upon, and valued as a person.

Although a mentor may have different reasons for helping you in the beginning, the friendship and intimacy that often develop can serve as a positive reason for continuing your relationship and for devoting increasing amounts of time to it.

A young woman described the professional and personal relationship she had with the advisor of a student organization she directed. "Virginia provided moral support for me, an unfailing sense that I could do my work.

"Our relationship was also a very personal one. She could see the value she was to another young woman. I believe she was less lonely as a professional because she could take a break from heavier duties and share on a personal basis with me. It was enjoyable for her to meet with me after a hectic or down day." No doubt this intimacy was at least one reason that her mentor continued her part of the involvement.

As a devoted mentee, you may bring out a side of your mentors previously hidden, similar to what happens in many love relationships. Your mentors may find that around you they can finally be themselves for the first time.

"For some reason, Sam brings out my good side," said Bill, the landscape designer who counseled his protege over pitchers of beer. "Maybe it's because he laughs at my jokes and asks the right questions, but I like the way I am around him. I can remember the profound quotes and jokes I used to tell years ago, and when I explain something to him it actually makes sense. I'm also more patient with him than I usually am with people."

Without realizing it, your mentors may see you as a substitute *child* or younger *sibling*. Playing a parenting role can be extremely satisfying, whether they've actually been real parents or not. If your mentors have children, they no doubt wish they could have been better parents in some ways, and you can help them to live out their ideal-parent fantasies.

The same holds true for mentors who think of themselves as ideal big brothers or sisters. "There was a certain sense of personal satisfaction from people coming to me, respecting my opinion," said an African-American woman. "No, not a certain sense, a great sense, and it made me feel good. I really liked the fact that to a certain extent, they needed me."

For several years, Grace managed a large textile manufacturing plant. She was a very supportive boss who took on a big-sister role with many of the men and women she hired and trained. In her case, this meant spending long hours counseling and drying tears, bringing people home for meals, helping to solve job-related problems as well as personal ones, loaning them money, even letting a few of them move in with her and her husband if they were in a bind. "They really needed my help, and I'm glad I was around to give it. I still get letters and phone calls from some of them."

In my original research, I interviewed a 70-year-old woman I'll call Maggie. She was a figure of great importance in what she called her "town," one of the largest cities in the U.S. Because of her wealth and wisdom, people looked to her when they needed help with everything from running a political campaign to getting a son or daughter into college.

"My interest has been in helping the person," said Maggie. "Sometimes it's with money, other times it's putting them on a committee that will get their name in the paper. People have talents, and providing an opportunity for them to spread their wings and do a good job, expressing what they have or believe, is the most satisfying thing in my

life. All the people of this town are like my
family, and I feel very close to many, many
of them." Maggie knew she was needed and
deeply enjoyed the crucial role she played.
She was greatly missed when she passed
away.

They're Resolving an Adult Ego Stage

Erik Erickson described a series of
"ego stages" through which all of us go. His
third adult ego stage, "Generativity versus
Stagnation," is one in which you either succeed or fail at leaving the last phases of
childhood behind and assuming full responsibility in the adult world. [6]
According to Erikson, you'll probably
be near age 40 when you enter this stage,
and as part of its successful completion,
you'll begin to care about the next generation in a new way. Serving as a mentor can
help you successfully resolve the stage in
favor of Generativity.
Many men and women in their mid to
late 30s wrestle with this stage, coming to
grips with what they want to do with the
rest of their lives. Many voice the need for
commitment, roots, and family ties they
previously avoided. One 37-year-old woman
named Sara told me, "In my 20s and even
my early 30s, I was totally immersed in
myself. I'm just now feeling ready to see

what I can do to help someone else have a better life. In a way, I'd like to help pave the way for the people coming after me."

In short, your mentors are motivated to assist you for a number of personal and professional reasons. This is what makes mentoring a marvelous two-way exchange.

The Motives of Your Mentors and You

Look at your list of past and present mentors, and think about all the good things each one gained from being connected with you. Beside each name, write a word or phrase that describes what you believe were (or are) the reasons that person had for helping you.

Were you doing some of their work for them? Serving as their crucial subordinate? Did you hire and pay them to help you? Were they being praised by their peers or otherwise recognized for helping you? Did you display loyalty to them and their causes?

Were you a key source of vicarious achievement for them? Were they investing in your future? Paying past moral debts by aiding you? Are you one of the underdogs they wanted to help? Were they enjoying an intimate relationship with you? Were they working through their ego stage of Generativity versus Stagnation?

Chances are you've had many reasons for helping mentees of your own. Think of the people you helped and why you did it—the real reasons. I think you'll agree that few human interactions involve total selfless giving. And that's okay, as long as neither of you is being mistreated.

Let's now look at what goes into the formula for your next successful mentoring relationship.

5

The Right Formula

*The good things in life are not to be had
singly, but come to us with a mixture.*

—Charles Lamb

To give you a taste of what makes a mentoring relationship work, I want to introduce you to one that didn't. See if you can identify what this well-meaning mentor did wrong.

Sara was eager to get to work the Monday morning after Thanksgiving. Off and on during the long holiday weekend she'd been thinking about her new staff member Kevin, a young business graduate. She'd been managing him for two weeks, but up to now she'd been so busy that she hadn't given him much attention. Kevin didn't seem to mind, but Sara was bothered. She'd do something about the situation that very day.

Kevin was a challenge. Twenty-eight, good looking, extremely articulate, sure of his abilities but with the right touch of modesty, he'd dazzled all the managers. As much as she wanted to oppose hiring him just to be different, Sara had to agree he was perfect for the job. Besides, she knew his father well and didn't want to have to explain her actions to him. The only weak points she could see were Kevin's extreme seriousness and the fact that he was, she felt, a little vague about his plans for the future. Now there was something she could help him with.

She felt a little intimidated by Kevin. Although Sara was determined to help him with his career, she wasn't really sure that he wanted any help from her. After all, she was only six years older than he and, as a matter of fact, he made a point of increasing distance between them. He always wanted to do everything his own way.

Sara asked Kevin to join her in her office right after lunch. She was a little nervous as she asked her secretary to hold her calls and told Kevin to make himself comfortable. She looked him straight in the eye and made her pitch. Kevin seemed a bit surprised when she described what she wanted to do for him, but he listened attentively and thanked her politely when he got up to leave. Over the next few days, Sara began playing the role of Kevin's mentor in earnest. She loaned him her private files, took him to lunch, rewrote his resume, gave him two mini-lectures on market research, and suggested that they co-author an article for the next company newsletter. Sara thought to herself, I wish I'd had this kind of help when I was getting started.

When interviewed later, Kevin described his reactions to this rush of attention from Sara. At first he was surprised and pleased by his boss's concern and help, and he stayed late that Monday evening to look through Sara's private files.

"What a disappointment they were," he said to me. "Instead of being helpful, they were incomplete and outdated. Most of the notes were rather petty remarks about some of the senior officials, and in fact I felt a little embarrassed reading them. The career goals she kept pushing on me were a far cry from what I wanted to do in the next five years, but I wasn't sure how to tell her that. She seemed so determined and pleased with herself."

The resume she wrote for him was, he felt, too gimmicky and even stretched the truth about his past. Her knowledge of market research paled in comparison to what he'd learned at Stanford and in past jobs.

"Yet she carried on like she was an expert. Again, I wasn't sure how honest I should be, so I kept quiet."

Sara's ideas to co-author an article for the company newsletter sounded all right initially, but after checking around, Kevin found out that almost no one read the newsletter, and those who did considered it only a mediocre effort. The main reason they looked at it was to see who could find the most typos. The article she suggested would take him hours to research, and he had other priorities.

Additionally, comments he overheard about Sara in the cafeteria let him know that she was seen by some people as a pushy, not-the-most-brilliant manager who was going nowhere in her own career. One woman warned him that he'd pay a price for Sara's help.

By the end of a month, Kevin had reached his limits. He didn't want to be rude, but the situation was becoming awkward. "I knew that Sara was trying to help, but I couldn't put up with it. I finally told her, 'Thanks, but I need to make it on my own.'"

Kevin applied for and got a transfer to another department, where he soon became the crucial subordinate of an aggressive young vice president. When I saw Sara again not long after Kevin transferred, she was still hurt by the way things had gone. "I couldn't believe how ungrateful this guy was.

He said he wanted to make it on his own. Talk about naive! My first attempt at being a mentor, and I totally bombed out."

Although most attempts at mentoring relationships are well intended, and the majority of experiences are at least moderately successful, some are doomed almost before they begin. Sara felt hurt and angry at Kevin's lack of appreciation and was frustrated by her inability to give him the right kind of help. Kevin was in a bind because he was being forced to accept help that he didn't really want or need.

Just what goes into a good mentoring partnership, anyway? How do you know whether or not yours has what it takes to succeed? The following key ingredients are present in relationships that make a positive difference in mentees' lives.

First Ingredient: Respect

Mutual respect is the first and key requirement for your relationship. Researchers James Clawson and M. B. Blank emphasize that respect and trust are musts for successful mentoring.[1]

Notice that I don't use the word, "chemistry." Although chemistry can enhance the picture and can be nice and even exciting when it occurs, powerful mentoring can occur *without chemistry*—as long as you and your mentor have strong mutual respect for each other.

You have to believe that your mentor has the status, skill, or power to help you before you'll willingly accept him or her in that role. At the same time, the prospective mentor must have a positive attitude about you. He or she has to think that you'd be a good investment and worth the time and energy it would take to work with you.

Mead knew Boas's reputation and ability as an anthropologist and believed he was a very able professor and potential sponsor. Jung recognized the status that Freud's name carried in European psychoanalytic circles and admired his work, so he willingly became his protege. Both mentors recognized the tremendous potential of their proteges early on and saw them live up to it.

Sometimes a mentoring relationship springs up involuntarily and then evolves into a mutually satisfying experience. Can you remember a time when you were turned off at first by a person who wanted to help you—and later found him or her to be quite wonderful? Or a time when a protege finally won you over? It's wise not to force mentoring relationships. You may have to let respect grow.

You'll probably respect your mentors most when they're highly knowledgeable and able to teach right from the start. Not all prospective mentors who are good at something can teach it, however. *Your task is to pull mentoring from the situation and to use some mentors as learning brokers to help you find more suitable teachers.*

Read Morgan W. McCall's excellent book, *High Flyers*, for ideas on how to develop respect and pull learning from situations, even from people who aren't very good teachers.[2]

It's a good idea to take a critical inventory of your own strengths and limitations to see how potential mentors may react to you. *Put yourself in your mentor's shoes and decide how much you'd respect a prospective mentee like you.*

Second Ingredient: Appropriate Mentoring

In order for your relationship to work well, you have to see the assistance offered as appropriate and valuable for you. If you see the help as outdated, superficial, or not worth the energy it takes to accept and use it, chances are you won't encourage the relationship, and it won't go very far.

Sometimes you have to judge the help not on the basis of its current value, but on the basis of what its *eventual impact* on your life will be. That's sometimes a tough judgment call. As you may have already discovered, sometimes you don't really appreciate help offered or received until later, in retrospect, when you see its effect on your life.

You may have to rely on your mentors' judgment regarding what and how much help you need at certain times, although with practice you'll be able to determine this for yourself.

Just as important as the kind of mentoring you receive is the *amount* of that help, and it's sometimes difficult for your mentors to know what's enough. In an effort to be helpful, they may push you too hard, give you too much advice, or watch too closely over your shoulder. If you balk at all the attention, they may pull back too far, leaving you on your own when you're not prepared.

The right dosage of help varies so much that you and your mentor will have to practice what behavioral psychologists call "successive approximation" in order to determine the right amount. This means that you'll have to gradually work up or down to the right dosage, sometimes going over and sometimes falling short of the ideal.

Third Ingredient: Proper Timing

Mentoring has to occur at the right time in order to work. This means where you and your mentor are in your own lives plus the specific timing of the intervention in your environment.

As Jackie told me, "I don't know what would have happened if I had met Kathryn three years earlier. Probably nothing. I wouldn't have been as ready to take on that kind of responsibility as I was when we did get together. In a way, timing was everything."

Psychiatrist Roger Gould, author of *Transformations,* points out that mentoring done at the right time can serve a legitimizing, permission-giving, empowering function that allows you to cross the boundaries between your "inner" systems (desires, needs, capabilities) and your "outer" systems of acting on these inner forces. But you have to be psychologically ready to make that crossing.[3]

Gene W. Thompson and Paul H. Dalton were probably the first to identify career stages, particularly within large organizations. Based upon their interviews with hundreds of engineers, scientists, accountants and other professionals, these researchers suggest that people go through four distinct stages in their careers. They tie into the need for proper timing in your mentoring relationships.[4]

Stage 1, *apprentice.* Here you usually work under the direction of others, even if you're not actually called an apprentice. You spend most of your time helping and learning from one or more senior personnel or mentors.

As an *individual contributor* in Stage 2, you have a considerable amount of skill and knowledge and work on demonstrating this competence, making your own contributions. You concentrate on developing a reputation as someone who's technically proficient and can work alone if necessary to achieve significant results.

As you move into Stage 3, *mentor*, you continue to contribute your technical skills, but now you're broadening and taking on more responsibility for influencing, guiding, and developing others. Chances are you've been doing some of this mentoring all along, but it increases in the third stage.

In Stage 4 you become an *organization influencer*, a force in shaping the future of your organization and perhaps your career field as a whole. You do this through negotiating and otherwise interfacing with the outside environment; developing new ideas, products, markets and services; helping to manage the resources of your organization toward specific goals; and assuming leadership roles in your field or in the society at large.

Depending on which of the above stages each person happens to be in, a potentially good mentoring experience can occur too soon or too late. For example, if one of your potential mentors is in Stage 3 (*men-*

tor) of his or her career development, and you're already in Stage 4 (*organization influencer*), the timing will probably be off, or the type of mentoring won't be what you need.

Sara was in Stage 3 when she tried to help Kevin. She wrongly assumed that since Kevin was new to the company, he was in Stage 1.

In addition to a good fit between the career stages of the mentor and you, the success of the relationship also depends upon timing in your environment. The events and conditions around you and your mentor can profoundly influence the nature of your experience.

Sara and Kevin's firm was in a period of decreased production and employee layoffs. Management was carefully watching all performances, particularly those of its most recently hired personnel. Kevin realized this and knew that he quickly had to establish a good reputation within the company. He didn't believe that linking closely with Sara was the most effective route for doing this.

The case of Sara and Kevin was a disaster on all three counts (mutual respect, appropriate mentoring, and proper timing). Sometimes only one weak component can ruin a building alliance. *If one ingredient is weak or lacking, a heavier burden is placed on the other two ingredients to compensate, and sometimes the relationship survives.*

For example, even if your respect for the mentor is less than satisfactory, the quality and quantity of the help may be so valuable that, together with the timing, it can make the mentoring experience a winner for you.

Louise and her mentee, Gary, are a good example of this situation. Louise was a highly successful person in the fashion industry, with a history of valuable and special contributions to the field. She had won every fashion award given, and the people who had been trained by her were certain to name their own salaries anywhere in the country.

Gary, who was just beginning his career, desperately needed this training. Despite the fact that he didn't care for Louise as a person and also hated to depend on anyone, he decided to accept the mentoring she offered. As a result of the exchange, he was able to establish a reputation for himself very quickly. Had the help been less valuable, or had Gary not been in Stage 1 of his career, the experience may not have been intense enough to have made it worthwhile.

Sometimes the timing is wrong, but the help is particularly desirable. Lori was a senior in college, planning to graduate the following June. During Christmas vacation she received a letter from her favorite aunt, who was going to spend the next five months in Paris on a temporary assignment at the

American embassy. The letter was an invitation to join her, all expenses paid, to study French and international politics under the aunt's watchful eye.

The timing was terrible, but Lori looked carefully at her alternatives, decided to join her aunt, and postponed graduation. She had a marvelous time, picked up some language and independent study credits, and finished one last course when she returned home that summer. She graduated in August, and since her French was so good, she got a part-time teaching job at the local community college and taught there while she went to graduate school.

Key Ingredients in Your Past Relationships

Now's a good time for you to analyze the ingredients of two mentoring relationships that you experienced in the past or are experiencing now. Choose one relationship that worked well for you and a second one that did not. Use the chart on the next page to analyze those relationships.

Try to decide how each ingredient—the respect you had (or didn't have) for each other, the quality and quantity of the mentoring help that was offered, and the timing of the experience—influenced the success of the relationship.

	Relationship Number 1 (Successful)	Relationship Number 2 (Unsuccessful)
Amount & Kind of Respect		
Quality & Quantity of Mentoring Help		
Timing - Careers		
Timing - Environment		
What I learned		
Any insights?		

You're almost ready to pursue some likely prospects, but not quite. First you need to know about all the hats your mentors can wear.

6

Roles Mentors Play

He that wrestles with us strengthens our nerves and sharpens our skill. Our antagonist is our helper.

—Edmund Burke

Your prospective mentors can play at least 10 different roles as they help you reach your goals. Let's take a look at what these roles are and how you can build a team of advocates for yourself.

Traditional Mentors

In the late 1970s and early 1980s, about a quarter of all visibly successful people, particularly those who were over 45 or who stayed in one organization for their entire careers, had what I call a *traditional mentor*.[1] In the 1990s, fewer people reported being assisted by this type of helper. In this decade, traditional mentors may start to disappear.

Traditional mentors are often strict, demanding individuals who expect a great deal from their proteges. In return, they go considerably out of their ways to help their usually younger colleagues. The relationships are almost always primary ones with strong emotional ties.

A company president described an incident with her traditional mentor from the early days of her career that typifies the bonding that occurs in these protective alliances.

"He couldn't go to a meeting, so he wrote the chairman a note and said I was going to take his place, that I'd be substituting for him. I happened to be sitting in his office when the chairman called and said there was no way that I was going to take my boss's place. In very polite language, Mr. Taylor told the chairman that I was coming and that I was going to represent the company, and he was going to accept it, period. He stood behind me many times like that and wouldn't let anyone push me around."

Traditional liaisons are often cross-gender (male-female) but usually platonic.

In fact, the proteges are frequently acquaintances or close friends of their mentors' families.

As one woman said, "My mentor in a sense was like a father. I knew the whole family, his wife and children, so I was like his daughter. I worked for him for 20 years, and he saw to it that I moved right along with him." Of course, human nature sometimes causes exceptions to these platonic male-female arrangements, and later we'll look at what can happen in those cases.

Although traditional long-term mentors still exist and can be the answer for some people, they seem to be a dying breed. Most successful people today are so mobile, independent, and adventuresome that *they don't want or need the old-time traditional mentor.* By their actions, they've helped to re-define the whole concept of mentoring and have made clever use of a series of the following "functional helpers" to suit their ever-changing needs.

Supportive Bosses

Without question, supportive bosses are the most common of all career mentors. Almost all successful people have had at least one or two such persons in their lives. This mentor is usually an immediate boss at work, but it's a role that can be played by anyone in a direct supervisory position over you, such as a teacher, coach, or project director.

While still a graduate student, Bonnie wangled an interview with Dr. Rollins, an expert on the topic she was researching. Their meeting was brief, but it left an indelible impression on her.

"Even though he was late for a plane and in a hurry, I was struck by how he gave me his full attention for the 15 minutes we had. I felt that I was foundering on the topic, but he made me feel very bright. He gave me some ideas and even loaned me a copy of his new book, which was still in draft form."

Bonnie never forgot that meeting, and its positive effect lingered pleasantly in her mind. Three years later, she'd graduated and was working on a project similar to the one she did in grad school. Her boss suggested that she contact Rollins to see what information he could provide, and she happily agreed. Bonnie lost no time in calling him to ask if they could discuss a possible collaboration.

Yes, he remembered her, and yes, he could meet with her, and why not talk over a Chinese dinner? Yes, there was a possibility that she could work with him as long as her job would still pay her salary. "He really didn't remember me from our first session," Bonnie confided, "although he swears he did. We figured out a way for me to work for him.

I saw this as an incredible chance to learn from him—he was one of my heroes—and at the same time get my work done."

Dr. Rollins quickly became Jim, and he began to play the role of Bonnie's supportive boss. He gave her almost free reign on her work, even though he was technically responsible for what she produced. He helped her with her research skills and bolstered her confidence every time she had self-doubts. The three-month project segued into a longer one, and before long Bonnie became just as important to Jim as he was to her.

Organization Sponsors[2]

These mentors are more difficult to find, for they reside in the upper echelon of management. In that position of power, they have a major say in deciding if you'll be among the chosen few promoted to these coveted ranks.

Unlike supportive bosses, organization sponsors don't stay in day-to-day contact with their proteges. Rather, they pull certain strings at crucial times but otherwise keep a certain distance. They share many characteristics with traditional mentors, but their physical location in the hierarchy gives them special definition.

One young executive, Marilyn, described the experience she had with two such mentors. For years, she worked on the staff of a small firm and served as a consultant to a larger company. During her consulting visits, two vice-presidents continually coaxed her to leave her firm and join theirs. They finally succeeded in recruiting her, and she made the move.

According to Marilyn, "They retreated on high after I was hired, but there was a tacit understanding that once I proved myself in my position, they would see that I was promoted. I saw one of them in the elevator a short time after I made the transfer, and he said, "Don't worry, we're looking after you." Marilyn quickly gained skills and experience and was promoted into middle management within a year.

Organization sponsors seldom advertise their roles or actions, but news of their mentoring spreads rapidly via a company's grapevine. Said a hopeful candidate: "One of the men, a corporate vice-president who's very influential, picks people he likes and puts them in the right hands. He hasn't said anything to me yet, but I've been told by persons here that I'm one of the people he likes."

As it turned out, this young protege had indeed caught the interest of the influential vice-president and quickly got the important breaks he was looking for.

Organization sponsors are difficult to acquire, but don't let that stop you from considering them as potential helpers.

Network Mentors

Network mentors are individuals who don't necessarily work where you do but who are a part of an informal or formal professional network. They could be members of a professional association such as the National Association of Female Executives (NAFE) or the American Bar Association. Some don't belong to an official association but are active in their fields and are willing to help people such as you.

In many ways, network mentors are the best possible mentors to find because they're committed to both career development of individuals and the furthering of their professional field. You speak each other's professional language.

An outstanding example of a network mentor is a woman I'll call Adrian, president of a national association's largest division. Personally and professionally, Adrian regularly goes out of her way to help less experienced men and women. She takes it upon herself to facilitate discussions of mentoring at national meetings of her association.

If you're starting or changing your career, it's important to plug into your professional association, especially at the local level. Potential mentees find it an enjoyable way to get exposure, meet potential mentors, and improve skills by taking part in programs presented as well as observing the experts around them.

Professional Mentors

Professional mentors make their living by assuming, at least in part, many of the roles just described here. Counselors can help you solve personal and career problems. Lawyers will fight your contract and tax battles. Agents will try to locate media attention or performance outlets for you. Members of the clergy can help you integrate your career goals with your other life values.

The New Yorker's Katherine White was a passionately devoted professional mentor who was greatly loved and admired by her writers. When she died, the magazine reported: "She gave to every writer she worked with a seemingly limitless amount of attention. It was is if there were no other writers. Yet there were scores of writers, and she managed to devote herself to all of them. . . she encouraged them endlessly, reassured them, comforted them, counseled them, mothered them."[3]

Not all professional mentors are that dedicated, but their services can help you if you choose them wisely. It may make sense for you to hire a professional mentor who can help you zero in on your goals.

As a licensed psychologist, I've been a professional mentor to hundreds of clients. It's been my privilege—and at times a real challenge—to help each person identify healthy goals and take steps toward achieving them. Without question, I've learned and grown tremendously from being a part of these mentees' journeys.

Patrons

Many now legendary musicians, artists, and poets were sponsored by patrons who were essential to their careers. Ludwig van Beethoven was supported by Count Ferdinand Waldstein and two Austrian princes, all three amateur musicians and philanthropists who believed in his ability and helped finance his work. Franz Joseph Haydn, one of Beethoven's teachers, was also supported by patrons, including Count Ferdinand Maximillian von Morzin and later the illustrious Prince Nicolaus Esterhazy. [4]

Michelangelo depended on the patronage of the Medici family. Even the young William Shakespeare enjoyed the patronage of the Earl of Southhampton. This system flourished undisturbed for centuries, and it was difficult for young artists to gain a foothold without the added luster of a prominent patron.

You may be surprised to know that the patronage system isn't dead. Its benefits can still be enjoyed by those who are shrewd enough to take advantage of them. Here's an example.

Wayne is a generous modern-day patron. He and his wife accumulated wealth from an import-export company they founded. They traveled all over the world, developing a large network of friends and contacts, and their house was always full of these foreign friends who came to visit them.

When his wife died, Wayne decided to sponsor a number of students from the countries he and his wife visited. He created several scholarships for foreign students at the college in his town and even provided room and board in his home for those who needed it.

Another patron described how she sponsored an artist she discovered at an outdoor art show in Santa Monica. "I saw his display from about a block away and knew immediately that he was going to be famous. I asked him right out if he needed a studio. My house is huge, and there's this sun porch in the back that I told him would be perfect. About a week later, he called and asked if the offer was still open. He moved in and started to paint immediately. He gives me paintings and teaches me about art, so it's not like I'm doing all the giving."

For you, patron support can mean anything from money to work space to room and board. If this is what you need, the right patron might be able to give it to you.

Invisible Godparents

Invisible godparents are perhaps the most unusual of all mentor figures. These are the "secret mentors" in some people's lives.

Although she didn't know it, such a mentor made arrangements for Sharon to progress in her career. Sharon only knew this corporate executive by name, but he'd seen some of her work and was impressed by it. He quietly contacted her immediate supervisor to suggest that Sharon be included in some important meetings and training programs. He also asked that his name not be mentioned.

Shortly after that, she was promoted from her secretarial position to that of research assistant, the bottom rung on the so-called professional ladder. When Sharon left the company, her invisible godparent kept informal tabs on her. Two years later, when he heard she was being considered for an important management position, he once again made an invisible gesture. Although her credentials and experience were excellent by then, the competition was keen, and this behind-the-scenes contact turned out to be the deciding factor in her getting the job.

Sharon neither discovered nor suspected this mentoring until six years later when she was a vice-president of another sizable corporation. One day she literally bumped into him and, much to her surprise, he called her by name and invited her to lunch. Over dessert, he finally admitted his secret involvements and, after her initial shock, they had a good laugh together.

Fortunately, Sharon's goals and the maneuvers of her invisible godparent happened to be compatible. Consequently, her belated discovery came as a pleasant surprise, and she began thinking of her phantom benefactor as a mentor. If her goals had been substantially different, and if she'd felt unfairly manipulated instead of aided, she wouldn't have considered him a mentor at all.

Invisible godparents aren't common, and you may never experience (or at least never find out about) this kind of mentoring in your life. They do exist, however, and you just might discover a silent helper somewhere along the way. Or you might be inspired to become one yourself in order to guide some unaware protege of your own.

Peer Mentors[5]

This group of helpers is made up of your friends, neighbors, and co-workers who are outside your family. Some of them can provide important mentoring support for your goals and plans.

"I was so delighted to find Anne," said a legislative aide on Capitol Hill in Washington, "because she's as ambitious as I am. We'll sit down and discuss the various pros and cons about a particular move, the risk versus reward, this congressman and that one. It's great because she'll look at the situation as I do—how we can position ourselves properly for the next right offer. I wouldn't consider making a move without Anne's approval."

An advertising executive I interviewed described a colleague in his former firm, a bright person who was obviously on the organization's fast track. After months of indecision, he finally asked this colleague's advice about whether he should leave the firm or stay.

"He encouraged me to leave because he knew that I had reached the point where I was stagnating in my job and becoming bored. He was fairly blunt about what he thought would happen if I stayed. At his prodding, I finally left, and it was the best thing I could have done. I started my own agency. Now I'm the boss."

A social worker who loves her job said that her best friend was the one who convinced her to go back to school and work on a master's degree full-time when she was 44. "I had no self-confidence at the time. I thought I could never compete in graduate school at my age, but she convinced me that I could."

Unsuspecting Hero Role-Models

This group is, in a way, the reverse of the invisible godparents. They're giving you help without knowing it themselves.

When I was just beginning to study the mentoring process, a woman named Donna wrote to me that Billie Jean King was her mentor. I assumed that she was a crackerjack tennis player, knew King well, and the two played tennis together regularly. We talked later, and I discovered that Donna didn't play tennis, had never met King, and hadn't even seen her in person.

"Billie Jean has been an incredible inspiration to me," she said, laughing at my surprise. "I've followed her career and her life for years. I read everything I can about her. I think she's a fantastic woman, someone I'm trying to be like. She doesn't know it, but I think of her as a kind of mentor."

In my early research, I met many other people who spoke of such heroes as their mentors. Who were some of these role models? John Kennedy. Jesus. Katherine Hepburn, Werner Erhard, Marlon Brando, Eleanor Roosevelt, to name just a few.

At first I thought this was stretching the definition of mentor. But examples kept appearing.

I've since learned that *mentees define who their mentors are.* I refuse to argue that these individuals are really role models—if mentees decide that the impact and definition—to them—is that of mentors.

You, too, can decide who your mentors are. At the same time, be careful with this term. Others may think you're missing reality and try to talk you into using a different word. A good compromise is to make these individuals part of your "virtual" development team and imagine what they would say to you directly.

Family Mentors

Can family members serve as mentors? Why not? If they fit any of the descriptions given in this chapter, there's no reason you can't identify them as mentors who help you reach your important life goals.

Most people point to their *parents* as being very influential on their lives and careers. Wolfgang Amadeus Mozart's father quickly recognized his child's incredible talent and abandoned his own musical career in order to take his son all over Europe to perform for exclusive audiences. (So anxious was he for his son to be impressive as a child prodigy that he nipped four years from the boy's age.)[6]

As is the case with most Olympic athletes, gold medalist ice skater Peggy Fleming had the around-the-clock support of her parents. For years her father accompanied her to 5:00 a.m. practice sessions.

A civil engineer's remarks about his father are typical. "My father influenced my life most. He taught me that second best was not good enough, and so I learned to give my best as a matter of course. He always told me that I should study hard and get a good education so that I could do what I wanted and be qualified for any job. I still listen to his advice carefully on all subjects."

Mothers can also be superb career mentors. In fact, the successful women in one study I conducted gave their mothers a slight edge over their fathers as the persons most influential at every one of their life stages.

As one woman put it, "My mother was the real mentor in my life. She not only made it possible for me to achieve what I have, but she also set a perfect example for my brother and me. I've always tried to be like her." Such diverse personalities as Jimmy Carter, Brooke Shields, and Bill Clinton obviously benefited from the powerful guidance of their mothers.

Grandparents also play mentor roles for large numbers of people. Many say that their grandfathers and grandmothers were the real mentors in their lives, perhaps because they were one step removed in time from them and had a broader, longer-range perspective on life.

One woman described her grandfather's help in this way. "He had a profound effect on my life. He died when I was 16, but up to that time he paid a great deal of attention to me. He always gave me the feeling that I was the most important person to him and that he expected great things of me.

"Although he lived a distance away, we corresponded frequently. He used to proofread and mark corrections on my letters and then return them to me. I never resented his corrections, probably because I was somewhat in awe of him. In many ways he maintained the leadership of the family, and I felt very happy to be the center of his attention."

A man I interviewed in some depth remarked, "My grandparents were always much more liberal and modern in their thinking than my parents were. They used to tell my mother and father to give me more freedom to learn things by myself. I used to love to visit them, because they would tell me about what they'd done, and they would say I could do anything I wanted when I grew up.

They'd come over from Hungary and started from scratch, so they knew what they were talking about. My folks didn't have to struggle all that hard, so they didn't stress that pioneer spirit so much."

In *The Person Who Changed My Life*, singer Gloria Estefan writes about her grandmother on her mother's side.

". . . Besides her obvious role as a grandparent, she represented to me a vivid example of a woman ahead of her time. She was a strong, caring, spiritual humanitarian who filled my life with possibilities and through her example gave me the belief that there was nothing I could not do or achieve in life. . . .

"The most valuable lessons I learned from my grandmother were to discover what makes you happy and do it with as much energy and joy as you can muster. And that success takes perseverance, determination, and an unwavering belief in what you have chosen to do. I feel fortunate to have found such an amazing mentor."[7]

Spouses can serve as mentors. A friend of mine, Evelyn, told me about the mentoring role her husband played early in their marriage. "He saw more in me than I saw in myself. He became my husband and mentor. He financed further education for me, took me all over the world, taught me to think big. He showed me that the successful life was the result of setting goals and working terribly hard for them. He taught me that whatever I wanted could be accomplished through believing, striving, and accepting."

Similarly, a young man talked about his wife. "She's someone I can go to and say, 'I've got this problem at work, and I think maybe I need your opinion to decide whether I'm on the right track.' She always listens and suggests some ideas. Invariably, after we talk I'm able to solve whatever it is that's bothering me." The two discuss almost every career move either one of them needs to make and seem to be excellent peer mentors for each other.

Sometimes *children* can play career mentoring roles for their parents. More and more of this is happening to women who are launching careers after their children are grown. Evelyn told me, "My daughter has been a role model for me lately. She, of course, is of a different generation with newer philosophies, and some of this has rubbed off on me."

Evelyn had separated from her husband about a year before I met her. Her daughter, who was also enrolled in a Ph.D. program and teaching part-time, had also recently separated from her husband. The daughter managed to handle the trauma of separation quite well and served as a shoulder and support system for Evelyn, who was shaken and lost after her own experience. Daughter encouraged mother to move closer to her and to go back to school, and now they're both working on their dissertations.

Changing Mentor Roles

The role played by a mentor can change over a period of time. For example, your manager may begin as a supportive boss and later be promoted and be an organization sponsor. If you eventually leave to start your own venture, this same mentor could offer to be your patron. It's important to know and influence what role you'd like him or her to play.

Mentor roles are changing in another way. The trend today is for everyone, including you, to develop skills in "career self-reliance." In his excellent book, *We Are All Self Employed*, Cliff Hakim advises us to change our paradigms about employers taking care of us and to take responsibility for our own dreams, goals, development, self-marketing, and satisfaction. It's only in doing so that we can pursue our dreams and find genuine passion in the work we do.[8]

This doesn't mean that managers, teachers, mentors, and other helpers are off the hook, however. Hakim emphasizes that rather than total independence, the ideal arrangement is strong *inter*dependence between our helpers and us.[9]

While mentors are valuable—and in fact critical for well-rounded success—*you should never count on mentors to make you successful.*

First of all, most would refuse. They're far too busy to orchestrate your life. (Look suspiciously at any who volunteer for such a controlling role.) Secondly, you know best what you want to achieve and the kinds of help you need to get there. Or you should.

Recognize that under this topic of changing mentor roles, typical mentors now expect you to do more for yourself and expect themselves to play a less intense role in your development than they might have a decade or two ago. However, you'll run into exceptions to this trend, so spend time studying your prospective mentors and discussing with them the role or roles they might be willing to play.

Now that you've seen the variety and scope of roles played by today's mentors, recognize that these relationships don't just fall into your lap. As a matter of fact, the competition for the best ones is stiff. Keep going as you learn specific ways to attract the right mentors for you.

7

Finding the Right Mentors

I would undertake to be an efficient pupil if it were possible to find an efficient teacher.

—Gertrude Stein

If you're like most prospective mentees, you now have two dilemmas: (1) you don't know any mentors personally who could provide the help you want, and (2) even if you did know someone, you have no idea how to approach him or her. Just how do you nail down a concrete arrangement for such a singular relationship?

Even if you swear that you have no likely mentor candidates, I'd like to show you how to find some. If you have one or two possible mentors in mind but don't know if they could really help, you can find ways to evaluate their worth before attracting their attention and help.

If you already have some choice would-be mentors waiting but have been resisting their help, it's time to give yourself permission to accept it.

People can be surprisingly passive or impulsive when it comes to receiving a mentor's help, and too little thought generally goes into this acceptance. You may think you should be extremely thankful for offers from any prospective mentors and should welcome any attention with open arms.

The truth is *you should choose your mentors very carefully*. Your task is to choose mentors who can help you define and reach your personal goals, not necessarily their goals—and certainly not someone else's—unless those goals happen to coincide with yours.

Here's a step-by-step procedure you can use to find the right mentors for you. If you follow it carefully, you'll be able to consider every option and every obstacle, and it should remove that last shred of hesitation you have.

1. Develop Your Own Personal Vision

Instead of thinking of people at this point, stop and think about your personal vision—*what you want to do with your life in the next one to five years.*

Experts on leadership, personal development, and career success are passionate about this important step. Kouzes and Posner, Stephen Covey, Warren Bennis, and others emphasize that crafting your very own vision will dramatically change your life.

I can't stress this point enough. Unless you create one or more *tentative* personal visions—pictures of those dreams—you may never reach them. Or other people will make major decisions for you, and you'll end up settling. If that feels uncomfortable, that's a good start.

Find a quiet uninterrupted setting, pull out some paper or your laptop, and start to draft your vision. If one vision sounds rigid, work on *three or four parallel possibilities*.

Picture yourself a year or two from now. You've achieved this exciting vision! Answer these questions in the *present tense*.

What are you like? What do the people you value say about you?

Who are the people you spend time with? What are your relationships like with each of them?

Where do you live?

How do you earn a living?

What do you own?

What's your leisure time like? What are you having fun doing?

What impact do you have on your community, country, or world?

Don't rush this process. Spend at least an hour alone, without interruptions, as you ask yourself these challenging questions.

If you take this time to be totally honest, beneath your verbalized vision are the things you *deeply value*. In order to dig down into your core values, ask yourself this probing question:

"If I have x, what does that bring me?"

For example, if you own a cabin in the mountains, what does that bring you? It gives you a place to see your family enjoy themselves . . . a spot where you can write your book . . . a summer retreat to which you can bring inner city kids . . . the realization of a dream your parents had but never reached, and so on.

Once you have the beginning of your vision, choose *one important aspect* of it.

2. Identify Three Critical Goals

Start thinking about *one to three goals* that will make that part of your vision actually happen. Take time to write them down, and make sure they're measurable. In other words, you'll *know* when you've reached them.

I've found in my research and training that wording your goals *as skills or competencies to develop* is a very practical and measurable way to make them happen.

List the most important *skills* you'll need. What skills do you now have that you could enhance, and which ones do you still need? For example, should you work on

- organizing yourself and your time?
- presenting your ideas in persuasive ways?
- listening to what people really say?
- planning and implementing complex projects?
- writing?
- managing people?
- becoming more visible?
- taking more risks?
- mastering the computer?

- setting priorities and saying no?

Give your skill list plenty of thought. First, you can probably meet some of your needs with *other resources besides mentors.* Instead of getting involved with a mentor, you could learn better with some classes, books, or Internet searches.

Second, even if mentors can help with the skills, you can't expect them to read your mind. Using your list, you can clarify your needs so that you'll know exactly what it is you're asking for when the time comes. *Make it easy for your mentors to help you* by presenting your needs in a clear and logical way.

Don't worry about the perfect goals. Just write down what you believe to be true, perhaps checking it with someone you trust. Later, you'll have a chance to get feedback from some of the mentors you select.

3. Evaluate Yourself as a Prospect

Are you a desirable mentee? Take this self-test. Read and rate yourself on each statement according to how much you agree or disagree with it. Circle 3 if you *strongly agree* with the statement, 2 if you *generally agree* with the statement, 1 if you *strongly disagree* with it, and 0 if you're *uncertain.* Be honest. Think hard about yourself as you are, not as you'd like to be.

Mentee Checklist

	Strongly agree	Generally agree	Strongly disagree	Uncertain
1. I've set some important goals for myself.	3	2	1	0
2. I know the kind of assistance I need.	3	2	1	0
3. I'm willing to accept help from a mentor.	3	2	1	0
4. I'm a good listener; I hear what others really say.	3	2	1	0
5. I'm a good follower when needed.	3	2	1	0
6. I can be counted on to carry out commitments.	3	2	1	0
7. I learn most new things quickly.	3	2	1	0
8. I'd be willing to speak up (diplomatically) if I disagreed with a mentor.	3	2	1	0
9. I'm good about thanking and otherwise showing appreciation to people.	3	2	1	0
10. My success potential is high; I'd be a good risk as a mentee.	3	2	1	0

Add up your total number of points. A score of 21-30 indicates that, based on your self-evaluation, you should be an excellent mentee candidate. You might even have several would-be mentors waiting already. If not, it's because they don't know about you.

A score of 11-20 indicates that you think you're good mentee material but could use a little more time to think through your abilities, your needs, and what're you're willing to do to meet those needs.

By making a commitment, carefully evaluating what you need and want, and then brushing up on your mentee skills, you should have no problem starting your search for some good mentors.

If you scored 10 or less, you should seriously question your desire to find a mentor at this time. Perhaps you're resisting help from others. If so, think about what your reasons are. How do you really feel about becoming a mentee? How can you maintain that balance between dependence and independence that you've worked hard to attain?

It was difficult for me, personally, to reach this balance. My parents died when I was 17, and I was determined to make it on my own. I really prided myself on being independent, and in fact refused to ask others for help for a long time. For years, I'd rather do without than turn to someone I knew. I'd pay a fortune for taxis when my car broke down rather than ask a neighbor or even a close friend for a ride.

I was always thought of as super competent by everybody. How could I admit that I couldn't do something and needed help? I was always afraid of being thought of as less than perfect, or worse, as a burden to others that they could reject. I think that was my worst fear.

It took a lot of persistent, caring friends and co-workers, plus some complex professional and personal situations, to finally convince me that it was okay to ask for help, that people were feeling distant from me and left out of my life because I was always the self-sufficient giver. They made me realize that I honestly gave them pleasure when they could help me out, and they didn't think I was a flake if I couldn't handle everything alone. If by some chance they couldn't help me at the moment, they'd tell me that, too. Now, even though I have to remind myself at times, I look for help when I need it.

If you allow yourself, you can ask for help, too. It's true that asking others for something involves risk, and you'll sometimes be turned down, even abruptly or rudely at times. You may get teased. But you'll succeed more often than you'll fail, especially if you approach the task in the right way. You'll be surprised at how often people will respond enthusiastically and how much you can learn and grow if you allow yourself to be at least a little vulnerable and dependent at times.

Is it difficult for you to take the role of receiving rather than giving help; being a follower instead of a leader; learning rather than teaching? If it is, consider some alternatives. You can find mentors who prefer to play a more directive role in the relationship, or you can experiment with a mentoring relationship and try these new behaviors. It might be easier than you think. Remember, it's only temporary.

4. Identify Some Mentor Candidates

Think once again about your goals, the kinds of help you require, and some possible helpers. Try to list more than one mentor for the same kind of help. Different approaches and viewpoints, even when they contradict one another, can be tremendously enlightening as you make your choices.

Now start to expand your list of people. Use your imagination, and think of anyone at all who might turn out to be helpful, even for just a small amount of information.

Here are some questions that you can ask yourself as you think of your candidates.

Who are the most influential or inspiring people I know?

Who could help me directly or get me in touch with someone who could?

Who thinks I have potential?

Who might think I had potential if he or she only knew me?

Is there someone who could accomplish his or her dreams with my help?

Who has recently "made it" who might be inspired by success to help me?

Who's carrying a tremendous load and could use some relief?

Who has helped me in the past and might help again?

What could my current boss provide?

You might find it helpful to make three columns: your goals and the kinds of help you're looking for, prospective mentors, and what you might contribute in return for the help.

Maybe you've thought of a few people who seem like they'd make good mentors, but you can't identify what they could do for you at this point. Put them on your list anyway, and see if you can learn more about them. Something about them might surface that will point to potential help.

Finally, take a long, hard look at your list. Here are some questions to ask as you examine each candidate.

Where are these potential mentors in terms of their own careers?

Are they just beginning, or are they perhaps switching career fields?

Half-hearted assistance from any one of them could have negative consequences for you.

How influential are your prospects? What offices do they hold? What honors have they received? In which inner circles do they sit?

Who listens to them, copies their style or adopts their opinions?

Check your library's copy of *Who's Who* (including the geographical versions) for names of people who are considered leaders in their fields. Study bibliographies of books and articles in your field of expertise. People who publish generally carry influence.

What's their current situation? Are
they in the middle of a crisis?

Put yourself in their shoes and ask if you
would be ready to help another person
(especially you) at this particular time. If
they're under a lot of pressure, that could
also lead to negative consequences for you.

Is there anything you could do to make
their lives easier right now and thus
turn the negative into positive?

Have these potential mentors helped
others? In what ways?

How do they feel about mentoring? Can
you talk to their former mentees?

Bear in mind that even if these potential
mentors haven't helped others, they may
still be able to help you. Perhaps no one has
ever requested their assistance before.

How do these potential mentors feel
about themselves?

It may be difficult to tell, but try to determine if they feel positive about their lives
and accomplishments. If they feel satisfied
with life thus far, you may reap some of
their enthusiasm. On the other hand, if your
potential mentors are dissatisfied with life

and the world at large, you may get very little mentoring.

> Have they accomplished quite a bit
> but wish they could have done more?

You may be the perfect recipient for some
valuable mentoring by providing a measure
of vicarious achievement. Be careful here,
however, because these mentors may heap
all their hopes on you and make you feel extremely pressured to succeed for them (one
of the risks of becoming a protege).

> What kind of relationships, if any, do
> you now have with them? Would adding
> the mentoring dimension have a posi-
> tive or negative effect?

> Is some mentoring already going on
> between the two of you that could be
> enhanced?

> If your relationships with them aren't
> very positive at the moment, were they
> once?

> How could they be rekindled? Is it worth
> trying?

> Why are you a better risk now than
> before?

Do you share similar goals and values?

It will be easier if you do. If they're very different from you but have a lot to offer, figure out ways to learn from and work around the differences for as long as the relationship can be valuable for both of you. Remember from Chapter 1 that today's mentees are smart enough to pursue mentors different from themselves in culture, race, gender, age, and style.

5. Prepare for Some Obstacles

Before you approach your candidates, do the same things you'd do if you were facing an important job interview. Find out all you can about their work, special interests, and needs. Talk to others who know them. If the individuals are public figures, do some reading in the library and on the Web.

Think through your request before you present it. Anticipate every possible question or negativism, and have responses for each. Once you've anticipated all the obstacles and thought through some creative ways around them, you're ready to take the plunge.

Your initial goal isn't a long-term mentoring relationship. It's a one-time informational exchange that causes your potential mentor to see you favorably and perhaps help you in some way.

6. Approach Your Possible Mentors

Would you like to know how others have contacted their mentors? Here are some tactics that successful mentees have used.

Diane Keaton auditioned for a play that Woody Allen was directing. Carl Jung wrote Sigmund Freud a complimentary letter.

A now successful screenwriter used a two-step approach to attract a television producer. She sent him a congratulatory letter when he was promoted and then followed the letter with a gift and note suggesting that they meet to discuss her script.

A student at a leading Eastern university wrote a heart-rending letter about himself and his need for funds to each member of the university's board of regents.

Several assertive employees I know phoned managers in their corporations and asked if they could confer with these managers for about 20 minutes to talk about decisions and goals faced. (Note that they didn't use the words mentor or mentoring.)

Ask others what they tried, and take careful note of the methods that worked and the ones that didn't so you'll have both sides of the picture. You may even want to talk to successful promoters, fund-raisers, salespeople, and anybody who has to sell himself or herself for a living and who asks for things from strangers as a matter of course. The object of collecting all these strategies is to make you as confident and unselfconscious as possible at the moment you make your request. The more natural it seems for both of you, the better the footing you'll establish, and the better your chances for a positive exchange.

Probably the oldest and safest strategy is to ask a mutual acquaintance to mention you to the potential mentor. If you know someone who can put in a good word for you, capitalize on that person's vantage. *Just be certain that you're seen as favorably as you think you are.* If you're not sure, ask for a frank reaction.

Proteges have taken other steps. A number join their potential mentors' clubs or associations. One of the most effective strategies is to volunteer to work on committees or task forces with prospective mentors so that they can see you perform.

Just like the prospective medical student, many write letters. This method can work, but bear in mind that highly desirable mentors receive many such appeals and won't have time to give their attention to all of them.

If you choose this avenue, try to compliment or congratulate the person on an accomplishment, and then share something about yourself that will spark some interest.

If you can think of anything that you might be able to do for him or her, by all means mention it. Include a sample of your work, if possible.

Andy wanted to make an impact on his potential mentor. He could have simply written the man a letter and asked for an appointment, but he came up with a more interesting approach.

The mentor was well known in his field and was published in various magazines. He had also received a fair amount of publicity, some of which was unfavorable. Andy decided to write a letter defending the prospective mentor's position to the editor of a newspaper which had made a few negative remarks about him. The letter was printed, and Andy sent a copy of it to the man, accompanied by a request for an interview. The prospective mentor could hardly say no.

When you're asking for a meeting, suggest 20 minutes. If your prospective mentor wants to extend it, that will be his or her choice. When you've succeeded in scheduling the meeting, never walk in cold. Decide what your desired outcomes are going to be, have a tentative agenda in mind, and make some mental or even written notes.

Take care to dress right (that means conservatively), and decide in advance what you will and won't say. Practice the meeting with a trusted confidante. Have that friend play it several different ways.

During your actual meeting, act the way you would act if you were already this person's mentee. Listen attentively, appear interested in his or her concerns, and agree to consider any advice you're given. Be specific in your requests for help, as illustrated by the examples below.

No	Yes
I don't know what I'd like to do.	I'd appreciate your reactions to these two ideas I'm considering.
Do you know anyone who could help me?	I'd like to meet someone who could help me get this published.
I need some money.	According to my figures, if I could locate a loan, or a series of loans, for $2,000, I could implement the first phase of this plan.

Follow up your meeting with an appreciative *hand-written* note. This is always better than a phone call, since the person can read it on his or her schedule. Write how much the visit meant to you, and try to comment on a particular thing said to you, such as, "For the first time, I actually understood what evaluability assessment is."

If your request didn't work out, analyze why it failed. Did you ask for too much? How was your timing? Did you select the wrong person? Did you clarify what exactly it was you wanted? Did you think of ways to make the experience beneficial for him or her? Did you come on too strong? Could you have been the 50th person that day to ask for something?

If you think there still might be a chance with this person, try another approach, or wait awhile before making contact again. But if anyone seems like a lost cause after the first meeting, chalk up the experience quickly, and try someone else.

As a final note, here's a list of important don'ts offered by successful mentees who were able to land good mentors.

1. *Don't use the words mentor, protege, or mentee when you're seeking help.* These loaded words will probably frighten someone who could otherwise be willing to help you but who doesn't feel comfortable being called a mentor or thinking of you as a protege/ mentee.

2. *Don't be too obvious or too desperate as you seek help.* If you seem too needy, a

prospective mentor may shy away, thinking that you're too big of a risk.

3. *Don't oversell yourself by excessive talking and a canned sales pitch.* Be ready to listen and adapt your requests to what you hear your candidates saying.

4. *Don't give up easily, since persistence might pay off.* Early ambivalence and even rejection might stem from a lack of focus in your message, poor timing, or information overload.

5. *Don't allow a lag to occur after the prospective mentor shows early signs of interest in you.* Move toward getting a commitment before he or she loses interest or becomes involved with someone or something else.

Additional details on finding appropriate mentoring are outlined in the booklet, *"Strategies for Getting the Mentoring You Need: A Look at Best Practices of Successful Mentees,"* noted in the References and Suggested Reading.[1]

Now that you know several strategies for finding the right mentors, you're well on your way. Before you approach those on your list, however, brush up on the new *mentoring etiquette* that's now being followed.

8

The New Etiquette of Mentoring

et-i-quette: *any special code of behavior or courtesy*
> — *The American Heritage Dictionary of the English Language*

Mentoring relationships now have their own etiquette. As with all forms of protocol or good manners, the purpose is to help you and your mentoring partners know what's appropriate and how to treat each other to prevent embarrassment and unintended slights.

Unfortunately, since this new etiquette is unofficial, it's often guessed at, ignored, or misinterpreted. Many mentoring participants end up, quite unknowingly, doing the wrong thing. Before long, mentees are dropped and don't know why. Mentors feel used and even burned out, vowing never to mentor again.

You can avoid all this discomfort if you and your mentors take responsibility to learn and practice some etiquette.

This chapter makes the "rules" more explicit.[1] These rules are actually guidelines, since all mentors and mentees come to relationships with different expectations, personal styles, and cultural traditions.

Ideally, one of the first things you and your partner will discuss is the protocol you'd like to use in your relationship.

As with all etiquette, the overriding rule is to make the other person feel at ease, knowledgeable about what to do, and valued as a person. In general, this means showing kindness, patience, flexibility, and appreciation, and using a combination of good business and social manners.

More specifically, here are several guidelines that have been followed in successful modern mentoring partnerships. Since mentees should show respect and—at least in the beginning—some deference to their mentors, the first set of do's and don'ts is for them.

Suggestions for Mentees

Be ultra-considerate of your mentor's time. Return phone calls and e-mail promptly (within 24 hours), be on time, and try never to cancel an appointment with him or her. Let your mentor be the one to suggest extra minutes or activities.

Listen attentively to all (or nearly all) your mentor has to say. Make appropriate eye contact when the two of you are meeting. Now and then look away and consider a point, so you don't seem to be staring. Try not to interrupt unless he or she talks for a long time and you need to clarify something.

Store what seems irrelevant for some future use. Don't tune out or try to change the subject when the topic seems unrelated to your immediate needs. Watch your body language; it may say you're bored even when you're trying not to be.

If you feel awkward, you may talk too much. Be complete yet succinct in your comments and explanations. Pause and use silence to gather your thoughts. Ask your mentor to give you clues if you're rambling.

By all means, ask for what you'd like from your mentor, yet be sensitive to his or her needs. Successful mentors are usually capable of saying no when they want to, but your mentor may feel awkward about disappointing you. If you sense the answer to your request is no, don't push, and accept the decision gracefully.

Seriously consider all advice you receive. Avoid "Yes, but." Show evidence you've used the help. Even if you choose a different alternative, point out how you used the advice to make your choice. If you forget to share the outcome of the help, your mentor will probably think he or she wasted time in giving it to you.

Show appreciation for every form of assistance your mentor gives you. Say thanks, compliment him or her privately and in front of others, write a short note. Don't take your mentor for granted or assume he or she doesn't need this positive reinforcement.

Make it easy for your mentor to give you corrective feedback. Ask for it early in the relationship. Again, watch your body language which may say, "I don't really want to hear this." Don't defend or explain yourself immediately. If the feedback is unclear to you, see if your mentor will be more specific and give an example.

Once the criticism sinks in and you've considered its merit, you may be able to give your rationale for using a different approach. Thank your mentor for being honest with you, and ask for suggestions on how to improve.

On the other hand, if your mentor tends to be over-critical and is harsh in delivering criticism, it's all right to bring up the difficulty this presents for you. It's doubtful that you'll change his or her basic style, but you may be able to get the message softened.

Assume the relationship will be strictly professional. Let your mentor take the lead in making the relationship more personal or friend-like. It may never develop in that direction. Don't intrude into your mentor's personal life or expect to be close friends.

Don't get romantically involved. Don't give the *appearance* of being romantically involved.

Make only positive or neutral comments about your mentor to others. If you disagree with your mentor's behaviors or values, share your perceptions directly with him or her. If the situation continues, consult with a trusted confidante on how to handle it.

Be prepared to move out of the relationship, at least the mentor-protege aspect, once you've reached your agreed-upon ending time. Keep the doors open to return to your mentor for advice or other help later. Leave on good terms, and keep in touch once you part company. Send a note or call from time to time to provide progress reports and say thanks again.

Mentors also have some rules to keep in mind. They, too, can take steps to show respect and put their mentees at ease.

Suggestions for Mentors

Help your mentee learn to manage the mentoring relationship with you. Mention your needs and any boundaries, such as time restraints. Explore his or her needs, listen to and suggest goals and topics to discuss, and ask if you can offer advice.

Respect your mentee's time as much as your own. Try not to assume, particularly if he or she is younger and less experienced, that your schedule always has top priority. Schedule specific times on your calendar to meet or otherwise help your mentee.

Don't make your mentee have to guess or learn by trial and error. Tell him or her what you expect such as: willing acceptance of this relationship on a temporary basis; thoughtful listening to your experiences and advice; genuine consideration of your suggestions, even if he or she ends up making a different decision; feedback on the usefulness of the mentoring you're providing; and prompt follow through on any task he or she agrees to do.

Tell your mentee what you're willing to give. Here are examples: your full attention during the time you're together; information on your specific job and your field; general advice on his or her plans and goals; and specific feedback and advice on your mentee's skills and situations.

Let your protege know what you don't feel comfortable providing, such as: job offers; personal recommendations or introductions to others (unless you decide later to offer them); extensive help with personal problems; and assistance that simply takes too much of your time (as judged by you) or that you don't choose to give for whatever reasons. As part of the mentoring process, teach your mentee what unreasonable expectations of mentors are.

It's always polite to ask if you can make a suggestion or offer criticism. Asking, "May I give you some feedback on that?" then waiting for permission usually ensures that your remarks will be received without defense.

Tell your mentee that you don't expect him or her to follow all of your suggestions. In that same light, remind yourself that your mentee is to move toward his or her (not your) goals. Don't expect a clone of yourself.

Express appreciation to your mentee for help given you or other steps taken. Avoid taking your mentee for granted or assuming he or she doesn't need positive reinforcement.

Recognize and work through conflicts in caring ways. Invite discussion of differences with your mentee. Talk about misperceptions or faux pas either of you commit related to gender, age, or cultural differences. If you get stuck, ask a third party to facilitate your discussion. Don't avoid discussion of potentially touchy subjects or force your solutions in conflicts.

Keep your relationship on a professional basis, particularly at first. Consider carefully if you want to encourage close friendship. If you push friendship in the beginning, then change your mind, your mentee could be hurt.

Don't get romantically involved or give the appearance of being romantically involved with your mentee.

In fact, avoid all unrealistic promises in the beginning and throughout the relationship. Because in many ways yours is similar to a counseling relationship, rejection by you (the counselor) can be difficult for your mentee.

Make only positive or neutral comments about your mentee to others. If you disagree with your mentee's behavior or values, share your perceptions with him or her directly. If the situation doesn't change, seek some help for the two of you.

Be prepared to end the relationship, at least the formalized mentoring aspect, once it's served its purpose. Be careful that you don't try to hang on to your protege indefinitely to meet your own needs. Have a closure meeting to discuss what you've accomplished together and how you'd like to define the relationship in the future. Keep the doors open for your mentee to return.

Whether you're a mentee or a mentor, being involved in this kind of relationship is a privilege for you. You should go out of your way to be gracious and thoughtful to the other person. When you're unclear about what to do or how to act, ask an expert, or better yet, ask your mentoring partner. The gesture of asking conveys respect for the other person, as well as for what the two of you are working to accomplish.

This guide to the new mentoring etiquette is by no means exhaustive, but it's a start. Use it as a *talking tool* for you and your mentor or mentee to come to agreement on how you'll interact.

Next, you're going to look at what happens inside your mentoring relationship as the two of you move through some interesting stages.

9

Inside the Mentoring Relationship

. . . there are companions and helpers along the way as well. One pilgrim may help another as when a blind man carries one who is lame upon his back, so that together they may make a pilgrimage that neither could make alone.

—Sheldon B. Kopp

Once you're involved in a mentoring relationship, what can you expect? Each one of your relationships is likely to be different in purpose, activities, length, and intensity. Yet, each will have its share of routine.

In general, you'll move through *stages* or *phases* in your longer mentoring relationships.[1] You can expect to see the following: mutual admiration, development, disillusionment or realistic appraisal, parting, and transformation. Let's take a look at each.

Phase I: Mutual Admiration

A memo from the vice-president states that you'll report to James Turbo for your next assignment. You have to interview a leader for a class assignment. You introduce yourself to the person on your left at a committee meeting. Somehow you're face to face with a budding mentoring relationship, and Phase I, Mutual Admiration, begins.

Once the relationship gets rolling, it often takes on many of the characteristics of parenting or falling in love. Each of you admires and has a highly favorable image of the other. You're both anxious to please, and you both give without being asked and without keeping score. You feel good about yourselves, good about each other, and good about your relationship. Mentoring is a wonderful thing!

The only negative note might be a slight feeling of uncertainty as both you and your partner fear possible rejection or disappointment.

Both you and your mentor typically present only your best sides during this phase. Shortcomings, when you notice them, are shrugged off and seem unimportant, particularly when you remember the stakes. You probably rush to defend each other in front of others who try to be critical.

If you're fortunate, something just clicks when you meet, an intuitive feeling that the partnership will be fruitful. Some would call this chemistry.

Bonnie knew from almost the moment she met Jim that she wanted to be his protege. She'd read his books and knew his reputation, but that wasn't the reason. She'd brushed up against other outstanding scholars before and felt no indication to try to initiate a mentoring relationship with them.

"When I thought about it later," she told me, "I realized it was because of several things. I could tell in the first few minutes we talked that Jim and I had the same basic philosophy when it came to helping people. I was also struck by his intensity. He was so alive, practically bursting with energy. I'd been around some very laid-back people at that time and was getting frustrated with their lack of direction. Jim seemed absolutely inspired, and I could feel myself catching it.

"I guess the best thing was the fact that he seemed to value what I said. He really listened to me. I was convinced that this was where I should be at this point in my life, and so I pursued the relationship."

Phase II: Development

When Jim and Bonnie's relationship began to develop, Jim did most of the obvious giving. He encouraged, taught, coached, assigned her responsibilities, and took her along to meetings and other events. "He really went beyond the call of duty for me," Bonnie said. "I thought I knew something about research, but I really didn't compared to him. He painstakingly went over every little step with me and was always encouraging. At meetings he'd always send some compliment my way either directly or indirectly."

Another protege in this phase expressed equally positive feelings about his mentor. "She's very good to me, and I in turn let her know that I know that. And we work very well together. Sometimes there's a master-servant element to it, and while there's a little ego resentment, I don't really care, because I have so much to learn."

Your mentor also benefits greatly from the relationship at this point, as he or she enjoys playing the part of the wise teacher, has you for a captive and willing audience, and perhaps is freed from some of the work that's been piling up. But you, the protege, particularly very early in Phase II, receive the most direct benefits. This is how it should be, although that will shift later.

As Jim and Bonnie's relationship continued to grow, the flow of help became more two-directional. Bonnie put it this way. "Well, at first everything Jim did seemed perfect. Once I got to know him well and also figured out what I was doing at work, however, I could see some areas where I could help.

"It got to the point that if he started to do something and I recognized that it wasn't quite right or up to par, I'd offer a correction or suggest an addition, or whatever. I felt a little more assertive and comfortable doing this as time went by, and I feel it's helped him in some respects. In fact, he told me he was glad that I was finally willing to stick my neck out and challenge him."

Confident that you're catching on, your mentor starts to delegate more and more responsibility to you and takes his or her teachings to a higher plane. You may talk organizational politics and games as trust builds between you, and you start sharing some confidences.

You spend quite a bit of time talking about career plans, especially yours, and the two of you probably assume that a great deal of career success lies ahead for you both. Much of the mutual admiration phase is still felt as your mentor shows pride in your accomplishments, and you in turn feel proud of your mentor's attention and approval.

The relationship may continue in this way for a considerable length of time. As one man put it, "There was always, I'd say, a line that I couldn't cross. Our relationship was boss and assistant." Several other proteges relate the same kinds of boundaries. "We always had a certain distance. I called him Mister until I left his office." "I respected her. She was always Miss Smith, and I *never* started calling her by her first name." "To this day, he's still Dr. Johnson to me."

Most relationships eventually develop to a point at which mentees are almost like peers, although such alliances seldom reach complete equality. As you, the mentee, gain knowledge, master skills, and learn to know your mentor's strengths and weaknesses, the original gaps between you begin to narrow, imperceptibly at first, and then with increasing speed and frequency.

However, the teacher-pupil framework is the bedrock of the relationship, and once it begins to change, the rest of the relationship also changes.

Phase III: Disillusionment/Realistic Appraisal

Once you've been helped to reach your original goals, your growth generally slows or even comes to a halt, and continuing the relationship in its original form can be counterproductive and disillusioning. It's then that a process of "psychological disengagement" begins.[2] This means that you begin to break free from the psychological dependence you have on each other. Yes, each other. Your mentor must also be willing to let you go.

One or both of you generally become unhappy as more and more shortcomings are recognized. Sometimes your mentor is the first to be disillusioned, perhaps because you're no longer seen as the ideal candidate for molding into the person he or she wants you to be. Similarly, you may begin to feel a bit impatient with the help that now seems old-hat or self-evident.

A mentor told me, "There are people who are really not going to make the effort to reach their potential. There was one fellow I tried so hard to help. He kept telling me that he wanted a chance, but when I would give him an opportunity to prove himself, he would never finish the job. He'd have a great excuse every time, but after a while I could see the game he was playing. There's a point where you have to walk away. It's hard, but you have to do it. Otherwise you end up taking all the blame yourself."

A high-powered book editor in New York mentioned how she was getting a little disillusioned with her old mentor. "I didn't ask his advice this time, mainly because he has gotten a little old and out of it, and I figured his advice wasn't useful. He doesn't seem to have any goals anymore, so how can he help me?"

As more time goes by, you can feel resentment building if you see your mentor as a block to your development. For example, Rob became the protege of his immediate boss, a financial expert eager to teach him about the economic aspects of manufacturing. Rob was a willing, grateful student and helper, and as his mentor moved up in the organization, he went with him as his personal assistant.

Finally, when the mentor became corporate treasurer, Rob became assistant corporate treasurer at the mentor's urging and recommendation. Rob was now an officer of the corporation with more status and perks. Later, again with the mentor's help, he became corporate secretary in addition to being assistant treasurer.

This new promotion caused a problem, since Rob's mentor ignored Rob's new responsibilities and acted as though Rob still "belonged" to him. Rob resented the little things his mentor was doing to disrupt his already hectic schedule, such as buzzing him to do tasks that his new personal secretary could easily do, not giving him some of the traditional responsibilities of the assistant treasurer's position, "forgetting" to tell him about a new regulation.

Although Rob sees himself as the future corporate treasurer, a position he wants very much, he's worried that he won't be ready for it. "It would be absurd not to be made treasurer. But I'm not trained at the moment. He hasn't groomed me or kept me aware of a lot of the things he's doing."

What neither Rob nor his mentor could articulate was that their mentoring relationship was in the normal phase of disillusionment. The mentor was dissatisfied because Rob was no longer willing to accept passively the demands and rules he'd always set down for him. This meant staying put at the assistant treasurer position until the mentor decided that Rob should be trained for the next step. The mentor was irritated that Rob was trying to strike out on his own instead of waiting and showing gratitude for all the help he'd received.

Rob was disillusioned because he didn't expect limits to be suddenly imposed on the mentoring he received. He wanted and expected his mentor to help him reach his final goal and was disappointed that it wasn't happening. He perceived a selfish side of his mentor that he hadn't recognized before. The two were playing psychological tug-of-war.

Levinson points out that your feelings toward your mentor may change from love, respect, and admiration to anger and resentment at whatever you see as hyper-critical and oppressively controlling behavior. In short, you may see that person as a "tyrannical and egocentric father [or mother] rather than as an enabling mentor."[3] Rob is still very fond of his boss, but while he struggles with this phase of the relationship, his patience is drawing very thin.

For years author Thomas Wolfe depended on his mentor-editor Maxwell Perkins to help him produce his best-selling novels.[4] He even dedicated *Of Time and the River* to Perkins as a public gesture of gratitude. Many critics claimed that Wolfe couldn't have written without Perkins, that Perkins was actually his "Svengali,"[5] and that Wolfe certainly would never have been able to publish a book without his mentor.

When Wolfe became aware of this criticism and started to recognize his own dependence on Perkins, he became extremely angry and was determined to break away from him. Author Marcia Davenport, an acquaintance of Wolfe's and another of Perkins' proteges, describes Wolfe's wrath in *Too Strong for Fantasy*. "Wolfe said, his loose lower lip dithering and his eyes wild, 'I'm going to show them I can write my books without Max. I'm going to leave Max and get another editor. . . .' He said that Max had kept some of the best parts out of that last book. . . . Over and over he said he had to get away from Max." [6]

This disillusionment phase is inevitable in successful mentoring relationships. Just as in romantic relationships, when you realize you're both only human, feelings of disappointment can be very strong. You ask yourself, "Is this all I can expect?" In romantic involvements, this awakening can be productive or destructive, depending on the commitment of the couple.

But mentoring relationships are different. With them, *disillusionment is always a good sign.* It's the first step toward what must eventually occur in a healthy mentoring alliance—a parting of the ways.

Phase IV: Parting

In this advanced stage, mentors and mentees begin to resemble parents and children more than lovers. In order for your mentoring relationship to be considered positive in terms of adult development, *you must break away from your mentor and achieve a measure of independent success on your own.*

This can occur in at least two ways. With longer mentoring relationships, it can tie in with the career stages mentioned earlier. As you move from apprentice to full-fledged individual contributor in your field, you must rely less on career mentors and more on yourself to open new doors and learn new skills.

With more modern, shorter mentoring partnerships, you should end the formal mentoring part of the relationship once you've met your agreed-upon goals. You may still keep in touch—or even move into an informal mentoring arrangement—but the psychological parting and formal severance are still important.

After years of working under Freud as the chosen "heir apparent," Jung began to feel trapped. Freud was insisting that Jung should concentrate on Freud's own research, preventing Jung from pursuing his own creative interests. Jung felt it was intolerable for Freud to stand in his way. To relieve his frustrations and have the freedom to work on his own, he had to break away. Freud was upset with Jung for leaving, even though Freud himself had taken the same step earlier with his own mentor, Josef Breuer. [7]

Sometimes the mentor makes the first move to end the relationship, especially when he or she is extremely disappointed. A woman I'll call Maria had been acting as a mentor for her assistant, Natalie, for close to a year. At first the exchange was excellent, and Natalie seemed eager to learn everything she could about the film studio where they worked.

After a while, however, Maria sensed that her protege wasn't sincere in wanting to grow. "I heard from several people in the department that Natalie was putting me down behind my back. When I started checking her work a little more closely, I found out that she was letting everything slide, missing key deadlines, covering up mistakes. When I confronted her, she refused to admit what she was doing. I finally withdrew my support and had her transferred. I just had to, because I didn't believe in her anymore. I really felt bad about that."

Occasionally a mentor or mentee is reluctant to end the relationship, and pain and bitterness result. Florence had one of these unhappy partings. She was the protege of a man who was very successful in retailing. He gave her priceless opportunities to learn the business from start to finish, and she learned exceptionally well.

After 12 years of steady accomplishments, Florence received a tremendous offer to go elsewhere, and she accepted. "He was very indignant when he found out that I was leaving. 'After all I've done for you!' he told me. He was nasty. In a way I suppose he thought he owned me."

Usually, however, the parting is seen as inevitable and in the best interests of both parties. Sheila worked in a small but prestigious firm for 17 years. She successfully climbed the ladder to vice-president and was the highest-ranking woman in the company.

Although she expressed a number of times a desire to become a partner in the firm, she was always refused. Finally her boss, whom she called her sponsor and with whom she had a close father-daughter relationship, recognized the block to her career development and urged her to look for an opportunity elsewhere.

"I was very fortunate to have a sponsor that said to me, 'Get out. You've gone as far as you can go. You get a good salary, but what's going to happen to you down the road? Think ahead 20 years from now. This is an age where women are getting promoted in business. You read in the paper about all these women and scream because your name isn't mentioned. It's because you're not working for a large firm. Get into one.'" Sheila took the step and headed for her goal.

In a similar case, Gavin was an ambitious young man who became a crucial subordinate to Leon, a corporate rising star. As Leon zigzagged from corporation to corporation, each time moving up the ladder, he took Gavin with him. Each move brought both of them higher salaries and more power. Finally, Leon became president and Gavin a vice-president of a major corporation.

Gavin was seen as "Leon's man," which he didn't particularly resent, at first.

But he was beginning to wonder if he could make it on his own. "It was getting a little ridiculous. If we were somewhere where we'd both have to be introduced to a group, it sounded as though they were reading the same resume twice." When Leon finally left that corporation, Gavin decided to make a move on his own. "We both decided it would be good to get away from each other for a while."

Gavin quickly found a vice-presidency at a Fortune 50 company and said he was very comfortable in his new solo role. "We may decide to work together again sometime in the future, but I think we both need to be on our own for now."

Another protege, Ed, also broke away from his mentor. "In my first job after college, my boss was the industrial relations vice-president of a large, multi-plant manufacturer. He was brilliant—an excellent speaker, scholar, salesman, skilled labor relations negotiator, communicator, and much more.

"For me the best part was that he was willing to share. He would philosophize, explain, teach, and encourage me to learn and grow. We had a delightful relationship for about five years, even though I always teased him about his fervent climb up the corporate ladder. He would laugh but kept saying that I'd take his place as company president one day.

"After about five years at the company, it hit me that I had no desire to be president or even a vice-president. I was getting more and more interested in my family, especially since my kids were starting school. I sat down with my boss one day and kind of reluctantly told him what I was thinking.

"At first he looked surprised and hurt, but after about an hour or so his face lit up and he started getting excited about what I was saying. It turned out that he really understood what I meant and suggested that I take a leave of absence for a year to try something else. I did, and that was 15 years ago. We parted as good friends and still keep in touch now and then. We're in two different worlds in a way, but we have a lot of respect for each other."

You and your mentor don't have to *physically* separate for your relationship to complete its cycle. In many cases, particularly with husband-wife pairs, proteges stay with their former mentors indefinitely. The parting is actually a *realignment* of the relationship, with the protege taking on a different, more independent role and the mentor withdrawing from the teacher role, both of them relating more as colleagues.

Bonnie and Jim had to wrestle with this phase of their relationship. He started as the typical supportive boss, but as their alliance evolved, they found they were falling in love. It was difficult for them, especially for Bonnie, to reconcile the two relationships. At first, she found herself letting Jim's influence in her business life affect her personal life as well.

This was irritating both of them, and finally they had a long talk about what they saw happening and how they felt about each other. Jim said he loved her very much but was tired of being her mentor. In fact, he needed some mentoring of his own for a change. At the same time, he recognized how quick he was to make decisions for both of them. He asked Bonnie if she'd be willing to risk taking the lead more often in their personal life and promised to pull back.

"I was so glad we had that talk," Bonnie said. "I guess ever since I was little I've had respect—too much really—for teachers and bosses and anybody over me. It was really hard for me to separate Jim-as-boss and Jim-as-lover. It was almost as if I needed his permission to do that.

"Well, anyway, we talked for a long time, and I gradually began to see where I was no longer the naive protege, that I had as much to contribute to him and to our relationship as he did. During that talk we kind of brought the mentor-protege thing to an end and really started concentrating on the romance. It's been great ever since, although we'll slip back into those old roles now and then."

Whether or not you and your mentor physically part company, at some point you must give up the security of being a mentee and move toward assuming the role of peer. In Levinson's words, "This kind of developmental achievement is one of the essences of adulthood."

Phase V: Transformation

In "Star Wars," wicked Darth Vader has his former teacher, Obiwan Kenobi, cornered and is about to take his life. He says, "The circle is now complete. When I left you, I was but the learner. Now I am the master."

After you and your mentor part company, the relationship moves in one of at least five directions. You can part and be forgotten, have an unpleasant separation, continue an informal mentoring relationship, get to know each other even better as friends, or possibly become your former mentor's mentor.

You'll be most easily forgotten when your relationships are secondary rather than primary ones. Most good mentors have so many mentees in a lifetime that it's almost impossible to keep track of everyone they helped.

You, on the other hand, will remember your mentors since you have relatively few and they touched some important part of your life. In fact, many of your former mentors will take on new importance as you reflect back upon your life in later years.

When I interview people in the second half of their lives, they usually don't recall much detail about their past mentors at first. As we continue to talk and explore, it becomes easier and even enjoyable for them to reminisce about these people and to put them in their true perspective, often for the first time.

If we have to stop our conversation and then meet again, they're even more enthusiastic at our next meeting. They're easily able to recall many of the personal encounters they had, the help they received, and what they learned about themselves and life as a result.

Now and then I find cases in which the wounds of disillusionment and parting never mend. Some mentors and proteges part very bitterly, determined not to make the same mistake again.

Freud had extremely bitter severances, both as protege and mentor. His split from Breuer was particularly full of resentment. For many years after their split, Freud would pass Breuer on the street and walk right by, pretending not to see him. Similarly, he was bitter about the departure of two of his own proteges, Jung and Alfred Adler, even going so far as to change the footnotes mentioning them in some of his writings.[8]

An attorney who became extremely disillusioned with her mentoring failures said, "I've just stopped doing it recently. I'm very turned off by young people because I've tried so hard to be a mentor to them and to help them. Maybe my judgment isn't any good, but I have struck out with every single person."

When we examined her past attempts, it was obvious that she held extremely high expectations for her intended proteges.

What's more, she hadn't told them what all those expectations were. They ended up groping in the dark because she didn't take the time to sit down and outline what she wanted. To this woman it was obvious what a good protege did (she had been an excellent one herself), and there was no need to explain what she saw as the obvious.

The third direction that your relationship may take is that of a more *informal* mentoring relationship. Once the intense, formal connection comes to an end, you and your mentor may continue on an informal basis. Instead of meeting and talking regularly, you simply check in with each other on occasion. As time goes on, it will probably be you who does the calling and updating.

As I mentioned earlier, good mentors have numerous mentees, and they can't keep up with all of them. It's a nice gift for your mentor if you decide to call or write now and then, both to say thanks (again) and to let him or her know you're doing all right and why.

A fourth possibility is that of evolving into a genuine *friendship*. An example is that of a dancer and two of her former teachers. She described how satisfied she is with the present state of their relationships. "Both of these men, by the way, are now very good friends of mine. In fact, whenever I'm in Chicago, we have lunch or dinner and talk about how our careers and lives are going."

Sharon, the woman with the invisible godparent, described her situation. "The relationship has changed drastically from those old days when I was the starry-eyed new kid in town and he was the wise old mentor pulling my strings from backstage.

"When he finally told me what he had done, we became close friends, extremely close in fact. It was fun because we laughed and giggled like two little kids over the things that went on in our two companies. His was much larger, and he had a tremendous amount of power, but when we got together you'd never know it. He continued to help me with a lot of my decisions for about two years after I discovered his help.

"About a year after we became friends, he started running into some heavy weather in his own career in terms of choices and changes that were going to be taking place, and suddenly he needed me as a career mentor, really as more of a sounding board and counselor. He had a tremendous opportunity but didn't know if he should go for it.

"We must have spent at least 24 hours talking about every last pro and con he had to consider. He finally decided to do it, and he said I really helped him decide."

Sharon's story illustrates the fifth possibility: *You might also act as a mentor for your former mentor.*

Like the people just described, you'll experience at least some of the phases of mutual admiration, development, disillusionment/realistic appraisal, parting, and transformation. Each stage can be rewarding and challenging for both of you.

Another Look at Your Relationships

As an application exercise, think back on all the mentoring relationships in which you've been involved, the same list that you assembled at the start of this book plus any new faces that have come to mind. Choose the one that was the *most satisfying* for you either as a mentor or a mentee. Now, mentally walk through that relationship and answer the following questions.

How did the two of you meet? Who initiated the relationship?

What were the early days like? Was there a substantial mutual admiration phase? How did you try to please each other?

As the relationship started to bloom, did the mentor provide most of the help? When did the help start to become more mutual?

When did you begin to become disillusioned with the other person or with the relationship? How did that feel? Did the two of you talk about this phase?

When did you end the formal mentor-protege aspect? Was it a physical or psychological parting or both? Who decided it was time? How difficult was this step for you?

If you're in a mentoring partnership now, what's your relationship like? Are you satisfied with it? What have you learned from this book to make it better?

If you answered these questions, you can see that every mentoring relationship is dynamic and changing all the time. Like any evolving relationship, it's subject to mal-functions. In the next chapter you'll take a look at some that could happen to you.

10

Potential Problems in Mentoring Relationships

*The biggest problem in the world could
have been solved when it was small.*

—Witter Bynner

By now you know that having a mentor or a mentee requires a lot. The disillusionment that can occur when either of you falls short of genius can be difficult.

Partings, even when inevitable and agreed upon, can be painful, particularly to the one who's left behind.

As a mentee, you've probably paid your share of dues for the benefits you've enjoyed in your relationships. This probably ranged from strains on your time to roller-coaster-like feelings. This chapter on problems isn't meant to discourage you but to add a measure of reality to the picture.

Any human interaction carries a certain amount of risk, and if you're aware of the possible pitfalls and are prepared to deal with them, you stand a better chance of avoiding serious problems. Here's a list of the most common challenges, along with ideas for handling them.

Excessive Time and Energy Commitments

Even the most casual relationships between mentors and mentees take time and effort; intensive ongoing ones can require a large chunk of both. Unless your mentors are unusually well organized or independently wealthy and looking for a new project to fill their long days, they're probably strapped for time with a list of priorities that puts you near the bottom. Even a phone call on your behalf takes several minutes; long mentoring sessions demand larger, more precious portions of their time.

Norma, a professor at an eastern university, was delighted when her prize student, Laura, came right out and asked her if she'd be her mentor. "At first I was a little taken aback at the term 'mentor,' because to me it had always meant a full-time guru or teacher or someone like that. I was much too busy to add that responsibility to my schedule, even though Laura deserved that kind of attention from somebody.

"After we talked for a while, though, I got the impression that Laura had a totally different idea of my role. She said she saw me as a kind of part-time advisor and critic, and it wouldn't take much time at all. I was flattered, really, because Laura is so bright, and several other faculty members were trying to get her for themselves. I wasn't quite sure how to be her mentor or how much time it would take, but we decided to try it.

"At first there was no problem. Laura would pop into my office now and then, ask a quick question or two, and then be on her merry way. But then it started. She began dropping in every morning, usually with doughnuts and coffee for both of us. She started asking my advice on this and that, wondering if I'd edit something she had written, asking me to phone so-and-so to see if she could get in his seminar, telling me about her boyfriend and so on.

"Finally, I just had to level with her and cut out most of the help I was giving her. She was hurt, and I felt guilty, and we never did end things very well. I can tell you one thing, though. I was a lot smarter the next time I got involved."

Time is only part of the sacrifice involved. A commitment to help you, unless it's a one-shot effort, demands a share of mental effort and risk-taking that can put a strain on even the most generous mentor. If your mentor is smart, he or she will ask again and again, "Are you worth it?"

As a mentee, you also devote extra time and energy. Your life is already full; a mentoring relationship will require one or two hours a month plus learning activities to schedule between mentoring sessions. Demanding and generous mentors can run you ragged.

A scientist described the relationship he had with his major professor. "For some reason he decided I was his heir apparent, and so he started inviting me everywhere with him to conferences, on business trips, to his home. My family and I would just be sitting down to dinner or going to bed and he'd call. 'You've got to come right over, there's someone you must meet' or 'I need your help on this problem right now.'

"He'd never look at the clock. I'd drop everything and run right over, flattered that he called me and not someone else. Then I'd bring home part of his work and stay up until all hours finishing it. My poor wife. She put up with it for a long time and then finally blew up at me. We almost got divorced over that man."

Solution:

Before you begin your relationship, decide how much time you're willing to spend on it. What restraints do you already have on your time? Which can be eliminated if necessary? How could you manage your time better? One of the unofficial rules is that mentees should be willing to spend at least as much time as their mentors, and usually much more.

My research indicates that as a modern mentee, you should plan to spend *at least four hours a month* on each of your mentoring relationships. This includes up to one or two hours in meetings with each mentor and another two plus hours working on assignments and projects on which your mentor gives you feedback. Do you have this much time and commitment?

Your mentor should decide if he or she has enough time to do what's needed for you. If not, he or she should pass on the opportunity, perhaps helping you find someone else. If you play the role of a mentor, define your time and energy limits, and make those very clear to your mentees. Remember that a mentoring relationship usually takes more time in the beginning than it does later on.

Pairs can stretch their available time by using the phone, fax, and e-mail to communicate and by including the mentees in calls, meetings, and other activities the

mentors have to attend anyway. To intensify learning, mentors and mentees should
always debrief these events afterward.

Use time and energy as monitoring de-
vices throughout your relationship. If your
mentor says that he or she is anxious to
help you but doesn't demonstrate any commitment by spending time with you or doing
something for you, it's probably a sign that
the relationship isn't a priority.

See if you can do something about it
by making sure you're available when and
where your mentor is and by bringing up the
issue. Be certain that your mentor continues to see you as a good risk. If this
doesn't help, talk about the issue. If necessary, move on, but leave gracefully, and
keep the door open so you can come back
later if you want.

If you're trying to be a mentor and
your mentee is always too busy for you, by
all means share your concern, and see if you
can find out why. If the reasons seem light-
weight and the sense of commitment shal-
low, you may be getting a message that your
help isn't really wanted at this time, and you
should move on.

Inappropriate Choice

Complications can occur when you
don't choose your mentors carefully. You'll
stand to lose valuable opportunities and

time if you end up with a mentor who isn't right for you.

Kevin and Sara, described earlier, were the classic mismatch. While Kevin didn't intentionally choose Sara as a mentor, he did go along with her plans and actions, at least for a while. Fortunately for him, he recognized quickly that Sara could do little for him. Worse, she might even jeopardize his career if he allowed the involvement to increase.

He managed to get a transfer to another department before much harm was done. His career didn't suffer from their brief relationship, and his frustrating experience even helped him get more serious about what he really wanted to do and finding mentors to help him do it.

If your mentors run into difficulties in their own lives, they may become so preoccupied that they either abandon you or pull you down with them.

That's exactly what happened to Marsha, a highly successful marketing director for a large manufacturing company. One day she received a phone call from Sherman, her former mentor-boss, who had helped her get started in her field 10 years before. Sherman was now struggling with his own new business and was desperately in need of help. On the brink of tears, he poured out his worries.

Marsha described the incident. "I asked him if he needed help, meaning could I find someone to help him. Unfortunately, he thought I meant me. 'Do you mean it, honey?' he asked, and just the way he said it, I said, 'Of course.' I felt that I owed him a lot for getting me started." Marsha turned in her resignation the next day and flew across the country to join him and help salvage his sinking business. Despite her gallant efforts, it folded in less than nine months, leaving Marsha unemployed and almost broke.

If a mentor moves to a different organization and invites you to go along, make sure you have an accurate picture of what your status will be in the new company. If you don't you might be in for an unpleasant surprise.

Conversely, as a mentor, you might find yourself saddled with an uninspired mentee. You, too, might be swept away by first impressions, taking on someone who lacks the ability or desire to learn quickly, or who soon turns a cold shoulder toward your aid.

My friend Sandra told me about her futile efforts to be a mentor. "We had a trainee last year, and I really tried to groom her. I went over things I didn't need to spend time with, gave her extra time to finish jobs, introduced her to all the VIPs. At first, she seemed interested, but after a while she started to get bored. She didn't give a damn about anything. In fact, she acted as if she were doing me a favor to go along with all my efforts."

Solution:

Don't rush. Take the time to do your homework before you become involved in a relationship. It's amazing how people will spend more time investigating a coffee maker than they will on a prospective mentor or mentee! Don't feel obligated to make a commitment to your very first prospect. Chapters 7 and 11 provide strategies for making a careful choice. Use them to prevent regrets later.

What if, despite the careful selection process, you discover later on that you goofed, that you made the wrong choice and know you shouldn't continue? How do you gracefully bow out of an unsatisfactory mentoring relationship?

If you've been honest with each other all along, you could be honest about your specific reasons for wanting to end your alliance. Focusing on your differences in style can be an easy and polite way of saying you have difficulty working together. Your other time commitments are another convenient and honest reason for pulling out. To keep the door open, say you'd like to keep in touch in the future, even if that seems highly unlikely at the time.

If you're in a formal mentoring program and aren't sure you're satisfied with your matched mentor, give the match some time. (I hope your program has a no-fault re-matching arrangement.) As a rule of thumb, meet at least *four times* with your mentor, and do all you can to zero in on something valuable you could gain from this temporary partnership.

Communicate your concerns to your program coordinator, and, if necessary, get another match. Always leave the door open to reconnect with your mentor down the road.

Unrealistic Expectations

Sometimes "wrong choices" are really unreasonable expectations. When you as a mentee are given too much responsibility too soon with little or no guidance or direction, you can struggle or even fail.

If you've established yourself in a field, you may feel pressure to continue in the same career, particularly if your mentors have invested so much time in you. You may hesitate or feel guilty about saying no to a generous mentor, even when the request contradicts your own goals.

A case in point is Scott, a former army captain and protege of two senior officers. Both of his mentors went out of their ways to train Scott and provide him with extra visibility. Both regularly expressed hope that he would make a career of the army, as they had done.

"At first I welcomed their direction and was flattered by their attention," Scott said. "But eventually I realized that I wasn't cut out for the military. The pressure I felt turned into guilt, especially since I'm sure I encouraged them and gave the impression that I had the same goals as they did far longer than I should have. I felt that by rejecting the army they would think I was saying that their entire life's work wasn't important.

"As the time came near for me to sign up again, these two officers really started to pour it on. We were in Vietnam at the same time. The one guy arranged for me to have an extra leave out of the country, figured out some excuse for me to go to Thailand. This was in addition to my R&R to Hong Kong, where I met my wife. The other one found me a really good assignment with him back in the States for my next tour. They kept talking to me about how great the benefits were, how young I'd still be when I finally retired.

"I finally had to tell them the truth, and it was the hardest thing I've ever had to do. I'd gotten a good offer from a big engineering firm in Texas, and I took it. I made it sound like it was really my wife's idea, that she couldn't take the military life. They were absolutely furious and couldn't believe I was serious about resigning my commission. They treated me like dirt after that until I left. They were real S.O.B.s."

The expectations that your mentors have of you may be extremely high indeed, enough to cause permanent scars should you feel that you've failed them in some way. Many of the proteges I've interviewed still carry the marks of the unrealistic expectations of their mentors.

Solution:

First, take a close look at exactly why you're feeling frustrated. Was he or she clearly a wrong choice? Or were your expectations of each other off base? What actually did you both expect?

In what specific areas did one or both of you anticipate too much? As a mentee, did you assume all your needs would be met by this one person? Did your mentor demand too much from you and expect you to be perfect?

Talk openly with your mentor about expectations, and try to do this very early, within the first month of your relationship. Since you're supposed to manage the arrangement, bring up the topic. Mention some of your hopes for the partnership, and see if they're reasonable expectations. Ask your mentor to be honest about his or her expectations of you and the partnership. Monitor these closely, and do "process checks" from time to time. See if each other's expectations are still reasonable after you've been interacting a few weeks.

Expectations of Failure

According to the Self-Fulfilling Prophecy mentioned earlier, you'll generally perform at the level people expect of you. Mentors who have high expectations for you might inspire you to achieve greatness. But what if the opposite occurs? When a so-called mentor halfheartedly assumes the role and deep down doesn't expect you to succeed, you could be starting out with two strikes against you.

Adult education expert Roz Loring described how we can actually cause others to fail. "It's like somebody giving you a recipe and leaving out the baking soda. That's often what happens. They leave out that one very valuable ingredient which makes all the difference. Mentoring, it seems to me, is when you really think through the whole thing and give all the things that are needed, that extra little spice."[1]

An example of the Self-Fulfilling Prophecy of failure is illustrated by one father who described how he had tried to "help" his daughter with her career. All during her senior year of high school, the girl talked about going to college in order to become a journalist.

"I really didn't think she needed to go to college," said her father, "since she wasn't that great a student and was probably going to marry her boyfriend in a couple of years anyway. I wanted to see her do something practical, like take business training, be a good secretary. But I went along with her talk. I told her I'd pay her way, even though I thought she was crazy and would probably flunk out the first semester. Sure enough, she did lousy and dropped out after about two months."

Little did he realize how clearly his message was received. In a separate interview, the daughter shared her feelings. "I wanted to be a journalist really badly. This was the one course I liked in high school. But my folks never thought I could do it, my dad especially. The look on his face when I'd talk about it made me feel like he was just humoring me. He said I could go to college if I really wanted to, but I could tell he didn't think I'd make it. He was right. I just didn't have enough confidence to hang in there."

This same challenge can occur with your mentors. If you expect them to fail or be nonhelpful, they probably will.

Solution:

If you have serious doubts about a potential mentee's chances for success, it's
generally best *not* to become that person's
mentor. Unless you're an incredibly good
actor, your doubts will cloud what you do
and say, and your mentee will suffer for it.
There's a slight chance that your negativism
could inspire him or her to do well "just to
show you," but this kind of negative inspiration gets pretty old after a while.

The kind of motivation I've heard mentioned most often by mentees is encouragement, a "you-and-me-against-the-world"
spirit that spurs proteges on against great
odds.

So examine your true expectations
about your prospective mentees. If you expect them to fail or do poorly, do them a
favor and stay out of their lives.

If you have nagging doubts about a
mentee with whom you're already involved,
be sure you give your best effort and help
him or her work on any weaknesses. Then, if
you still think the outlook is bleak, help your
mentee find some other source of help. If he
or she is determined to succeed, there's no
doubt that someone, or a number of some-
ones, can work wonders.

Be optimistic about your mentors. If
you expect them to be successful—and help

them help you—success is more likely to happen.

Protege's Feelings of Inferiority

A poster for the New York School of Visual Arts shows a melancholy clown gazing at the stars and bears this inscription: "To be good is not enough, when you dream of being great."

When you're exposed to successful mentors who seem to have everything, your expectations and goals for yourself will probably become greater. The problem is, if you don't achieve equal success, you may become discouraged and depressed at your relative "failure." Even if you do very well compared to others, you could remain disappointed with yourself.

The success of your mentor might, in fact, make everyone appear disappointing in comparison. One young woman told me, "My mentor was so successful, famous, handsome, and kind that it's been extremely hard for me to be objective about the men I meet now. None of them comes close to him. I almost regret that I met him, because I probably won't find anyone quite that good again. I won't be that successful either."

Even though the relationship with her mentor was totally platonic, she was having difficulty relating to other men socially or romantically. She, like many who experience the loss of a loved one, completely idealized her mentor and wouldn't give anyone else a chance.

Solution:

The easiest way to avoid this kind of disappointment is to change how you judge your successes. Most of us use a "norm-referenced" measurement to see how well we're doing. That means we compare ourselves to the group of people that we think is average, or the group that appears to be most like us.

This is the kind of scale that was used to evaluate you in school. All the standardized tests you ever took compared you to thousands of others in your age group or grade. It's also the measure that your parents used when they compared your size to that of your brother, the neighbor's child, and whatever size Dr. Spock said was typical for your age.

Using that kind of measuring stick, you'll *always* find individuals who are more successful than you. If you're just starting out in your career, it's natural to notice only those people who are more skilled, talented, and successful. Some of them may seem to be light-years ahead of you.

If one of these super people happens to be a mentor of yours, the gap between where you are and where he or she is will seem virtually impossible to close. In comparison with your mentor, you can feel inadequate and judge others that way, too.

Fortunately, there's a better way to go about it: the "criterion-referenced" instead of the norm-referenced approach. Simply stated, you use *yourself* as the measuring stick. With this method, you set specific goals for yourself and then decide, after a designated period of time, how well you've progressed.

This is the strategy schools use for individualized or self-paced learning. It's also popular in the business world, where workers set their own objectives to meet during the next performance review period and then are rated and rewarded on how well they meet them.

Frankly, it may not work for you. To help, use what cognitive psychologists call "cognitive restructuring" to stop, change your old thoughts, and begin thinking this new way.[2]

If disappointment with yourself compared to your mentors and other successful people continues to be a problem, try this alternate approach. You'll find support from a lot of happy people who traded in their old measuring sticks.

Unfair Manipulation

When you perceive that your mentors don't have your best interests in mind, or that they're unfairly manipulating you for their own gain, your adult development can be negatively influenced.

According to Levinson, "A mentor only serves my development through the particular character of the relationship we have. If a mentor is only interested in how much work I produce . . . and if I perform well, and then he or she helps me to advance, my advancement is being facilitated in terms of a career . . . but my development isn't. In fact, one of the main things I may learn from that relationship is that he likes me if I serve his needs, and he's not interested in me at all if I don't. That doesn't further my successful adult development."[3]

I believe this is mainly true when you feel unfairly manipulated by a *primary* mentor. Since your relationship with this person is usually based on a great deal of trust and dependence, the discovery can hurt.

The situation is different with your secondary mentors. Because your relationships with them are usually more business-like in nature, you may feel a little more willing to be manipulated—even a little unfairly—if you know what's happening, you're gaining a great deal from the encounter, and the experience is fairly short in duration.

Mentors can also feel manipulated and used. A friend, Sam, related his story about a protege whom he felt took unfair advantage of him. Sam works full time as an actor but developed an avocation in antiques and art objects. He's very successful at buying and selling old Asian rugs, American brass, and other collectors' items.

In the course of his travels, he met Grant, a younger man who was extremely interested in working for Sam and learning the antique business. For the next couple of years Sam groomed his protege, teaching him the intricacies of the field. The two did well financially, and they split all commissions and shared new information equally, or so Sam thought.

Sam told me about his rude awakening. "I ran into one of our regular customers, who told me that he paid Grant a certain price for a rug. That price was 50 percent higher than Grant reported and divided with me. When I did a quick check on some other sales, I found out that Grant had cheated me dozens of times.

"Needless to say, I was furious about the money, but I was even more upset that Grant had deceived me like that." Sam was cynical about mentoring relationships and swore that he'd never get involved in one again.

Solution:

If you're starting to feel manipulated or think you're being taken unfair advantage of by your mentor or mentee, take a close look at what's going on between you. Make an objective list of what you think you're giving to the relationship and what you're receiving from it.

Keep in mind the cycle of the relationship (mutual admiration, development, disillusionment/realistic appraisal, parting, and transformation), and determine who's giving what, how much time is involved, what each is sacrificing, and what your feelings are as a result. Try to write your partner's portion from his or her perspective, not yours.

Decide what you're intentionally or unintentionally contributing to the problem. Have you, for example, volunteered to take on extra tasks? Have you tacitly approved when the other person has said or done something you disliked or resented?

Do you *appear* to enjoy the present balance or lack of balance? Have you made your needs known? Have your needs changed or increased since the last time the two of you talked about them? Have your partner's needs changed?

Once you've taken a long, hard look at the situation, set aside a time for an uninterrupted discussion with your mentor or mentee and decide, beforehand, some tentative outcomes that would satisfy you. Write some notes. They'll help you remember what to say.

Chances are good that you'll find patterns that both of you want to alter. If, on the other hand, you're alone in your feelings and your partner sees no need for compromise, you're faced with a tough decision.

If you stay involved, you'll have to work on becoming more assertive about your needs, and you'll have to make your limits very clear. If not, your resentment will fester and will probably destroy the relationship.

Excessive Jealousy of Mentors or Mentees

It's thrilling to watch a mentee develop and become successful, knowing that you've contributed to this special growth. Yet some mentors find their proteges' success threatening.

A successful architect told me about the strained relationship she had with her husband and former mentor, also an architect. When they first met, he painstakingly taught her most of what he knew about his work. In time they married, and she took a leave of absence from her job for a few years to stay home and care for the two young sons from his first marriage. He repeatedly coaxed her to return to work and finally arranged for a live-in nanny to care for the boys.

"It was good to get back to work at first," she explained. "I found that I could pick up where I left off and, in fact, I was doing much better than I'd done before. Glen started urging me to take some of his jobs out of state since he was so busy, so I began making presentations all over the place.

"Well, it was funny. Pretty soon the different customers started asking for me instead of Glen. I also won a design award about that time. At first Glen was proud of me and used to brag about me to friends when we'd go out. After a while, though, he wasn't saying as much, at least not as many positive things.

"It was even worse right before I'd leave on one of my business trips. He's say that he hoped it would go well, but he'd get very distant and not even kiss and hug me or say he'd miss me like he used to. If I'd phone from wherever I was, he'd act like I was disturbing him and cut the conversation short.

"I started dreading those trips and even turned some down because of the strain it was causing. I'm not *sure* it was jealously on Glen's part, but I think that was what he felt."

If you have more than one mentor at a time, they may become jealous when they learn that they're not your exclusive influence. A case of *inter-mentor rivalry* could occur, and you might have to juggle dates and stories as you try to please everybody.

This situation happened to me. In my first job, I worked for two bosses. The two of them liked each other, but I found that underneath their camaraderie there was a strong competitive edge.

In the beginning, I openly shared with each one what the other had taught me. It was fine for a while, and they both seemed to accept what the other offered. As our relationships progressed, however, they each began to question and criticize the things I confided. It finally got so intense that I decided not to breathe a word about the mentoring I was getting from either of them.

Once your mentoring relationships mature and you become more competent and self-assured, you may start to feel jealous of your mentors. Particularly in the disillusionment phase of long-term relationships, you may see yourself as someone who is just as capable as your mentor or even more so.

Jealousy can set in as you become irritated about the prizes your mentor receives from the world while you still toil unrecognized. Either of you can feel hurt or resentful when the other pays attention to outsiders.

Solution:

All of us feel jealous or envious about something at some point in our lives, and a certain amount of jealousy is probably inevitable in mentoring relationships, given the close nature of these involvements. Mentally prepare yourself to experience at least a small amount. For example, you can expect twinges of jealousy when you see your partner shooting ahead.

Jealousy can be a real problem, however, when it's carried to extremes. Rarely, fortunately, some mentors become terribly possessive of their proteges and allow them no other helpers. Also, some proteges are overcome with jealous feelings and sabotage their mentors' work or other relationships.

Psychologists generally agree that jealousy thrives on lack of self-esteem and self-confidence. Theoretically, if you feel terrific about yourself and are absolutely sure of yourself in every situation, you almost never feel jealous. On the other hand, people who lack self-esteem or who are unsure of the commitment someone has made to them often draw attention to themselves to purposely cause feelings of jealousy in the other person.

Once again, take a close look at your relationship. If you're feeling jealous, try to figure out why. Is your partner acting in ways to provoke you? Or are you misinterpreting his or her behavior because you're feeling down about yourself?

If he or she is doing better than you are, is it because of greater ability or greater effort? Remember, mentoring relationships aren't destined to continue past a certain point. Mentors are supposed to work themselves out of the role, and proteges are supposed to eventually break away.

If your partner is feeling jealous about you, what are you doing consciously or unconsciously to provoke those feelings? What could you do to help your partner recognize his or her self-worth? You can't make someone self-confident, but you can certainly help by finding areas in which he or she excels, giving due praise, and helping him or her create a more realistic and positive self-evaluation.

Discuss jealous feelings with someone you trust, not necessarily your mentor or mentee. You can keep jealousy to a minimum, if both of you keep communication open and agree to some ground rules.

Excessive Jealousy From Others

The other people in your life outside the mentoring relationship can also become jealous and put varying degrees of pressure on you. Your spouse or close friends may become suspicious of the time and attention spent on your mentoring partner. Because of pressure from home, your mentor or mentee may temper his or her publicly expressed enthusiasm for you, especially if you're of opposite genders.

Even if you're the same gender, gossip about your relationship can occur. You may be teased by your peers and envied or resented by those who haven't been able to develop their own mentoring relationships. Most mentees report feeling uncomfortable when their status is first recognized by their associates.

One woman explained what happened when two of her managers collaborated to see that she got a significant promotion. "The old secretary to the president was absolutely hysterical about the whole thing. She was really upset, and she got all the girls to hate me. I mean, no one would even say good morning to me. It was really hard on me because these women had been my main friends for years. We shared a lot of things, not only about work but about our families.

"When they started ignoring me and then making smart remarks, I could hardly take it. It was really the worst month of my life. It took me a long time to adjust to the new job and to them. It still isn't very good."

Such resistance and conflicts aren't unusual among people who had to suffer through many years of discrimination and hard work before they reached their po-

sitions of power and then suddenly encoun-
tered younger employees who wanted to
make their way speedily up the executive
ladder.

These seasoned individuals recognize
the fact that if they were beginning their
careers today, the opportunities for advancement would be greater than those that
existed before. Understandably, some of
them resent the new breed. They may particularly resent those who have influential
mentors. To make matters even worse,
these mentors are sometimes the managers
of these older employees.

This peer resentment and jealousy can
be carried to extremes. Ruth is a dynamic
African-American who became the executive
vice-president of her company partly because of the efforts of her mentor, the president. She described the price she had to
pay. Several of her former peers became so
jealous of her new status that they deliber-
ately started doing annoying things. They
would telephone her house at all hours of the
night to harass her and her husband.

One afternoon the jealous women played an even crueler trick. "They called the
funeral home, and that's when it almost
killed my husband. I was gone and my kids
were down the street playing. The doorbell
rang, and my husband went to the door.
These undertakers were standing there.
They had their stretcher out and were about

to come into the house. They said they came to pick up my son! My husband was a wreck until he found the kids. They were still down the street playing, of course, but he didn't know that at the time."

A melodramatic example? Yes, but it really happened. Jealousy is one of the most difficult problems you may deal with, so be prepared for it. The lengths to which people will go if their emotions get out of control are always unpredictable—and sometimes harmful.

Solution:

The same strategies you use for coping with jealousy inside your mentoring relationships can be used to counteract similar feelings of the people outside of them. In this case, you and your partner will be the "common enemy," the joint recipients of the jealousy. If the people mean little to you or your partner, it probably isn't worth spending much energy on the issue. But if they're important to you, try to determine how you might be provoking the situation. Have you been ignoring these other people or hinting at your preference for your colleague's company?

In many organizations, employees who didn't participate in formal or informal mentoring partnerships in the past are starting new initiatives to make mentoring available to more people. For example, instead of resenting formal mentoring programs for exempt employees, many non-exempt employees are starting programs for themselves.

Look closely at your relationship with your mentor or mentee, and recognize what that relationship is to you. *Should* others in your life feel threatened? Monitor your relationship at all times to be sure that your behavior is what you intend.

Overdependence

Mentors and proteges can easily become too dependent upon one another. A classic case of the consequences arising from a protege's dependence on a mentor is that of Wolfe and Perkins.[4] Although he was also mentoring other famous writers at the time, including F. Scott Fitzgerald and Ernest Hemingway, Perkins devoted vast amounts of time to Wolfe. Editing the author's lengthy, rambling writing and putting up with fluctuating moods was difficult and extremely time-consuming.

Word got around literary circles that Wolfe's dependence had grown to oversized proportions. The persistent rumor was that none of Wolfe's works could have been written at all without Perkins. Even though Wolfe himself had fueled the fire by writing a passionate dedication statement to Perkins at the beginning of *Of Time and the River* and making remarks during their 10 collaborative years, he became enraged when he learned of this public criticism.

After several abortive attempts to leave Perkins and Scribner's, he finally broke away in order to prove to himself that he could survive without his mentor. The irony is that Wolfe died shortly after this, and Perkins was named the executor of Wolfe's estate. He ended up overseeing the editing and publishing of Wolfe's last works, even though his former protege was under contract to a different publisher.

While Wolfe was much more dependent on Perkins than Perkins was on him, the editor felt very deeply about Wolfe and was hurt by his departure, especially by the way Wolfe ended their involvement. Perkins confided in Wolfe and spent many pleasant hours drinking and talking with his friend. They shared a powerful interdependence, and the parting took its toll on both of them.

While most proteges are rather dependent in the early stages of the relationship, many, like Wolfe, find it difficult to ease out of this dependent state.

Mike, a Hollywood agent I interviewed, related a particularly harrowing experience he had with his protege-client, a well-known actor I'll call Darrell. When he was discovered by Mike, Darrell relied on his agent to make nearly all his decisions from which roles to take to the wallpaper to put on his apartment walls.

At first Mike enjoyed the responsibility and felt important and needed in this very personal role. But as time went by, Darrell leaned more and more on Mike for praise, reassurance, advice on all his personal problems, and even companionship.

Mike told me, "I started feeling uncomfortable both for myself—I was being swallowed up and had to ignore my other commitments—and for Darrell. I felt he wasn't ever going to take responsibility for his own life. At the same time, I was getting a lot from the relationship and didn't want to lose it entirely."

The difficult situation came to a head one dramatic night at the actor's beach house. Both had been drinking, and Darrell had had quite a bit of cocaine.

Mike suddenly heard a scream from the balcony that jutted out over the rocky beach below the house. He went running out to the balcony, where he saw the actor teetering back and forth on the edge of the narrow railing. "Save my life, Mike!" he shouted. The agent froze in his tracks, assessed the situation, and came to a split-second decision.

He walked away.

Darrell finally stepped down from the ledge. "For the next few minutes he called me every name in the book, and then he sat down and cried," said Mike. "But his over-dependence on me finally stopped."

Tensions can increase as mentors fret about what will happen when their mentees become confident enough to manage without them. Proteges may wonder when they'll find themselves replaced by more promising new-comers or what will happen when they finally face the world on their own.

Since most don't know about the pre-dictable cycle of mentoring relationships, they're often shocked when the end looms near, and they sometimes hang on long after a break is needed.

Solution:

As you've seen, the cycle of the rela-tionship calls for greater dependence of the mentee on the mentor in the beginning, followed by gradual interdependence and fin-ally by more and more independence on the parts of both mentor and mentee. Knowing about this predictable process and the fact that the relationship is temporary should make it easier for you to avoid becoming overly dependent. Sharing this information with your mentoring partners will help them with similar concerns.

Look at your feelings about depen-dence. Do you like to be taken care of? Or do you prefer to avoid dependency at all costs? Do you get a lot of pleasure from looking after someone else? How do these general feelings apply to your past or present mentoring relationships?

Is it obvious that one or both of you are leaning too heavily on the other for advice or emotional support? Are you depending on your mentor's judgment of your performance instead of your own evaluation of your work? Discuss these concerns with your partner.

Interact with more than one mentor or mentee at a time so that you don't rely totally on one riveting relationship. Maintain other involvements and activities outside your mentoring relationships. Share decisions and tasks with your partners so that no one gets over-dependent.

Build your self-reliant attitude and behavior. For example, instead of always relying on your mentor to judge your work, try to internalize some of his or her standards, mix in those of other knowledgeable critics, and then set your own criteria. Go easy on yourself, and enjoy some rewards when you succeed.

Romance and Sexual Involvement

Although romance and sexual intimacy between mentors and proteges don't spell automatic disaster, difficulties almost always occur when relationships take this turn. I have no statistics on the subject, but these involvements occurred in the past and will continue to go on regardless of the consequences.

When I began my research, I found them to be much more common than I originally anticipated. Proteges have become romantically involved with every kind of mentor—supportive bosses, peer mentors, patrons, and organization sponsors. Long-term, "traditional" mentor-protege relationships usually remain platonic, although even these sometimes take romantic twists.

Romantic liaisons can be casual and pleasant and end without complications, with no one getting hurt. On the other hand, serious problems can arise when the emotional involvement is intense. As Sheehy warns, "The woman may have a difficult time finding her own equilibrium because her professional, emotional, and often her sexual nourishment as well have their source in the same person."[5]

Adele and her mentor are a good example of the problems that can emerge from this kind of involvement. Adele took great pride in the fact that she had always attached herself not to rising stars but to powerful men who had already become successful in the business world. She became the eager protege of several such men (at different times) and reveled in the reflected glory and power that these associations brought her.

One of these men was especially attentive to Adele. He taught her all the tricks of the business, took her with him on glamorous trips, and saw to it that she was promoted to officer rank in the company. Adele fell deeply in love with this mentor-boss, and soon the two of them were heavily involved as lovers. They began talking of marriage, even though he had yet to initiate his divorce.

Little by little, the relationship began to become more important to Adele than anything else in her life. The time the relationship took and the demands of her lover put a strain on her career and even on her health. She pushed herself harder and harder at the office in order to do her usual excellent work. Others in the company started to suspect what was happening, which increased the pressure on her even more. She couldn't resign, as she thought the job was fascinating and the pay was good. Yet she was growing more and more dependent upon her mentor-lover to provide both professional and emotional support.

Suddenly, one day the mentor left both the company and Adele without a word. With the help of tranquilizers and a therapist, she managed to hang on to her job and muddle through, but she was devastated by her lover's desertion, and her physical health suffered. Several months later, she was still upset and totally confused about who she really was, what her career meant to her, and where her life was going.

Solution:

The problems related to romance and sexual involvement may be the most complex and the most difficult. Most books on career-life planning and management development advise strongly against getting romantically involved with your mentors or proteges, and for good reason.

Romantic involvement can hurt your career if others find out, if you become overly dependent on your partner as a result, or if you find yourself relying more on your personality and sexual attractiveness than on your career-related skills.

As I've advised numerous times already, closely monitor what develops in your mentoring relationships, and continue communicating about it. If you feel yourself starting to fall for your partner, step back—actually get away from each other—and get a perspective on what you're doing and feeling. Declare a moratorium on seeing each other long enough to decide what you both want to do. Consider all the factors, and make some wise decisions.

Mentors and mentees use various strategies to prevent romance from happening. Some make a point of always meeting their partners in settings that discourage any physical contact. Most concentrate on developing emotional intimacy and romantic relationships *outside* the mentoring alliance so that they don't have to look to their mentoring partners to satisfy all their needs. Some finally choose to end the relationships.

If you're already romantically involved with your mentor or mentee, you still have some choices. Again, determine your most important values, needs, and priorities. Analyze your alternatives, and communicate your concerns to your partner. You have to decide for yourself, and the more active you are in your decision, the more satisfied you'll feel with yourself and the way you handled the situation.

To sum up, you face many potential problems in mentoring relationships. Not all of them will happen to you, and you may skip every challenge. These potential hurdles shouldn't discourage you from pursuing mentoring. *The rewards you get from these partnerships are worth the price you have to pay for them.*

11

Becoming a Mentor

The best advisors, helpers, friends
always are those not who tell us how to
act in special cases, but who give us, out
of themselves, the ardent spirit and
desire to act right, and leave us then,
even through many blunders, to find out
what our own form of right action is.

—Phillips Brooks

Satisfied proteges almost always become mentors at some point in their lives. As you consider becoming a mentor yourself, take another look at what you've experienced up to now.

Reflecting Back

Think once again about your past mentoring relationships that worked well and also those that didn't. As you begin to pull together some ideas for what you'd like to do in the future as a mentor, you can glean some guidelines from what happened to you.

Which actions were most successful for you and them?

Which didn't work out well and why?

Think of the best mentoring relationship you ever experienced or observed.

How was it initiated? Maintained? Ended? How were problems resolved?

What would you like to live over if you could?

Some Mentee Types

As you recall your experiences and look around at mentees that you know, including yourself in the past, you might recognize one or more of the following types.

The Reluctant Mentee. This person hesitates about accepting help from you. This could be a first-time experience for him or her. It's possible that the reluctant mentee isn't convinced of your value or intent. He or she may find you a little intimidating.

The mentee may be getting special help from another mentor and is reluctant to be "unfaithful." Once the mentee sees the value of the mentoring you can provide and knows how to proceed, it's very possible that he or she will become interested in you and even be enthusiastic about the relationship.

The Inexperienced Mentee. This individual wants a mentor but isn't very skilled in how to carry out a mentoring relationship. He or she may push you too hard or not hard enough. The person could be late to meetings or forget to do homework you assign.

You'll have to take the lead with this mentee, teach what you expect, and show him or her how to manage a mentor.

The Overeager Mentee. The overeager mentee idealizes you and is determined to please you at all costs. There's a chance that in the effort to please, the mentee may hesitate or refuse to disagree with you even when doing so makes sense.

You can become very flattered by the attention of an over-eager mentee. What's more, you'll probably end up spending far more time than you ever anticipated on the relationship. You'll have to speak up and help this mentee learn how to work with you.

The Manipulating Mentee. This individual knows exactly what he or she wants and is willing to go after it even if it means taking unfair advantage of you. In most of your interactions, this person will only look out for his or her own interests. The mentee may know a lot about the mentoring process and will use that knowledge to over-control your relationship.

You can reinforce this mentee for showing initiative, but you'll need to look out for your own needs and push back at any unfair requests. Let this mentee know your reactions so he or she can improve.

The Ideal Mentee. While no single ideal mentee will match the needs, characteristics, and expectations of every mentor, certain mentees have a number of characteristics that appeal, at least to the mentors I've studied.

"Ideal" mentees have goals but are willing to consider or at least listen to other options. They're willing to learn from anyone who can teach, and they learn quickly and well. They value loyalty but are willing to challenge their mentors when called for.

They're reliable and prompt, complete assignments, and aren't afraid to take the initiative in new areas. They're enjoyable to be around.

With these mentees, your job is to reinforce their attitudes and actions, teach them all you can, and help them successfully continue on their ways.

Looking Ahead

Now you're prepared to do some planning for the mentoring you're going to do in the future. Here are some suggestions to help you choose mentees and begin the process.

1. *Be clear on what your motives are for helping.* If you're not sure yourself, potential mentees are bound to get mixed messages from you.

2. *Analyze what you have to offer prospective proteges.* Be honest with yourself as you consider what skills, knowledge, or other contributions you could make. Acknowledge, too, where your weak spots are and what you aren't able to provide. If you're not an expert in the skills your potential mentees want to develop, you can still serve as a learning broker and help them find the right assistance.

3. *Attend to your mentees' needs, but consider your own as well.* Be certain what you want from your relationships, and set boundaries as appropriate.

4. *If potential mentees resist your help at first, don't give up right away.* They may not recognize the value of what you have to

offer or may not be sure of your motives. Persistence to a point could help.

5. *Consider taking on proteges who may differ from you and have something to teach you.* It's always easier to help someone like yourself, but take a risk and try cross-difference mentoring. You'll learn a lot.

6. *Even if you aren't overly enthusiastic about helping particular individuals, try to develop interest in them.* Give the candidates the benefit of the doubt. If you can't change your attitude, see if you can find them more willing mentors.

7. *Exchange plenty of information.* When you're starting out, ask your mentees to share some history, plans, and goals. Share your own story, including what drives you, what you do for a living, what you like about your work, the paths you took to get here, what you wish you'd known earlier, your mentors and what they gave you, funny incidents, how you've combined your work and the rest of your life, and some of your mistakes.

8. *Study what motivates your mentees' actions.* Praise? How much? What kinds? When should you give it? Watch how each mentee responds to reinforcement by others. If you're not sure what kind to use, ask.

9. *Encourage your mentees to ask questions.* For many cultures, asking questions of an authority figure such as you is wrong, disrespectful, or at least very intimidating.

10. *With your mentees, set some specific goals and activities for your partnerships.* Start with two or three measurable goals, monitor progress, and perhaps add more later. The goals should be based on your mentees' needs, preferably some skills or competencies to develop.

Then come up with some good *learning activities.* For example, if you're helping someone try for an upcoming job opening, the two of you can strategize an approach, work on a resume, practice interviews, replay weak sections, etc.

11. *Come up with ways to evaluate the success of your relationships.* Ask your mentees very early, "What would make this a successful partnership for you?" Come up with some measures, regularly check on progress, and make shifts whenever you need to.

12. *Work on enhancing your mentoring skills and those of your mentees.* Over the past 23 years, I've identified the following as critical *core skills* needed by both mentors and mentees:

- listening actively,
- identifying one's goals and current
     reality,
- building trust, and
- encouraging.

When you're in the *mentor* role, your additional skills are:

- inspiring,
- giving corrective feedback,
- managing risks (protecting your
     mentee from disastrous errors),
- opening doors, and
- instructing/developing capabilities.

When you're in the *mentee* role, you'll utilize these additional skills:

- acquiring mentors,
- learning quickly,
- showing initiative,
- following through, and
- managing a mentoring relationship.

Seek feedback on your skills from others who'll be candid with you.

Ideally, your mentees will acquire other good mentors besides you. Help them build their mentee skills so they can be competitive in today's mentor market.

If you'd like to measure your mentoring skills on a more formal basis, see the Mentoring Skills Assessment (MSA) listed in the References and Suggested Reading and published by MindGarden. The MSA provides objective feedback and personalized tips on all 14 of the above skills.[1]

13. *Be prepared for Departure Day.* The successful mentoring cycle requires your mentees to eventually leave the shelter of your protection and make it on their own. If you've done your job well, including helping them come up with other mentors, they could in the process surpass you. They might not even look back, although they, like you, will always remember their mentors' help.

By now you have a good idea of how to be an effective mentor. In case you want to help others—or your organization—develop effective formalized mentoring, take a look at the next chapter. You'll learn how mentoring is being used in several new ways.

12

Becoming a Mentors' Mentor: Mentoring in Organizations

There are two ways of exerting one's strength. One is pushing down, the other is pulling up.

—Booker T. Washington

Once you've had a positive experience as a protege and then as a mentor, you may wish that other people could experience the same kinds of wonderful relationships.

If you want to help others succeed with mentoring, you can do this. Use your

strength to pull others up by becoming a
"mentors' mentor" for your company, professional association, community group, or
other organization.

The idea of planned mentoring really
caught on in the early 1990s. It's now an
important complement to the informal and
spontaneous mentoring that was always
there—but only enjoyed by some.

The U.S. government has formalized
mentoring for at least three decades. Programs exist in the Internal Revenue Service,
Federal Executive Development Program,
U.S. Army, the Small Business Admin-
istration, and many other agencies and
departments. State and provincial governments as well as city agencies in the U.S.
and Canada have started mentoring initiatives for their staffs.

In the private sector, formalized men-
toring is well-established in such corpor-
ations as Hewlett-Packard Company, Agi-
lent Technologies, DuPont, Enron, FedEx,
AT&T, Kimberly-Clark, Texaco, Lockheed
Martin, State Farm Insurance, Lucent
Technologies, PricewaterhouseCoopers, and
Houston Lighting and Power.

Countless colleges, universities, school
districts, health-care agencies, and religious
organizations offer mentoring programs for
staff, faculty, students, and other audiences.

Each of these mentoring efforts is *planned* in that individuals help people link with more experienced helpers rather than waiting for them to find each other on their own. The planned efforts have goals, structure, a set of strategic interventions, and a way to evaluate what's taking place.

The main purpose of planned mentoring is to equip people for new roles or levels of responsibility. Instead of leaving this critical process to chance, the organizations pave the way for success.

Mentees like the process because it's an officially sanctioned way to increase self-confidence, gain skills, and avoid big errors. Mentors find it enjoyable to help motivated individuals succeed, learn from mentees, and often get recognition for volunteering.

Organization leaders favor the process when they find that mentoring participants demonstrate increased loyalty and commitment to the organizations, and turnover decreases. Individual performances and the quality of goods and services they produce often improves. Companies find they have a competitive edge in hiring or recruiting when they offer applicants a chance to work with mentors.

Mentoring programs make it possible for mentors to provide mentees with one or more kinds of mentoring—advice, instruction, coaching, encouragement, modeling, inspiration, visibility, corrective feedback, and opportunities to perform—all mentioned earlier in this book.

Should Your Organization Try Planned Mentoring?

Before you launch planned mentoring in your organization, take plenty of time to investigate and decide if this is the right intervention to use. It may make more sense to use other development strategies and wait until later to try anything new with mentoring. (Remember, spontaneous or informal mentoring is going on all the time.)

In order to decide, pull together a team of people interested in mentoring. Interview many individuals throughout your organization and in similar organizations. Ask individuals and small focus groups about their receptivity to the idea of formalized mentoring.

Here are some questions to ask yourself and other planners who are considering the wisdom of initiating a formalized effort.

Who's backing this idea and to what extent?

As with any major improvement effort, planned mentoring must be supported from the top down. If top leaders want the process to occur, it will have a better chance of succeeding than if they're neutral on the idea. (If they're against the idea, don't go any further until their receptivity changes.) Will the leaders' verbal support be backed up with their own time investment, and financial support to cover at least a part-time coordinator, participant training, materials, printing, and other costs?

What's our current organizational climate?

If your organization is experiencing financial problems, layoffs, large-scale reorganization, or other challenges likely to take time and affect morale, the setting and timing probably won't be right for planned mentoring.

On the other hand, if your organization is financially solvent, leadership is supportive, the target populations for the program are eager, and the organization isn't overloaded with other "programs," the timing and situation could be right.

What will the goals or purposes of the mentoring effort be?

Be clear on the intent. Is it to develop knowledge and skills of promising managerial candidates? If so, how was this development done in the past? How receptive are people likely to be to the use of a new approach?

Is the effort aimed at meeting affirmative action or diversity goals? This isn't necessarily wrong, but how do the target audiences feel about the strategy? How will you manage the reactions of ineligible individuals? Will the activities be seen as only a token effort for a much larger problem?

Is it to get senior managers and other professionals to pass on their skills and the organization's values and traditions? If so, do these individuals want to play this role? Do they have time, and are they skilled enough to do it?

Will the program help new hires enter the organization more smoothly? Help new managers learn their jobs? Are you certain you have enough mentors to do this?

Planned mentoring can have legitimate purposes other than these. Be clear on the intent you have in mind.

How have comparable efforts succeeded in the past?

What's the recent history of other efforts to change and improve the organization? Which ideas were well received and carried out? Why did they succeed? What can you learn from those experiences? Which ones ran into strong resistance or were dropped for lack of interest? Again, what can you learn from these efforts for the proposed mentoring initiative?

What are the practical restraints we face?

Will mentors and mentees have time to work on their goals? Do you and the rest of the task force have time and energy to organize and carry out the project? Do you have a reasonable budget?

If we do this, how formalized should we make the effort?

The answer to this question will probably follow from the previous questions. To help you think through your options, consider the following *continuum* of strategies.

A Continuum of Strategies

Picture a line with *informal*, totally unplanned mentoring to the far left. This is the "natural" or spontaneous mentoring that has always gone on. To the far right is a *formal* mentoring program with matched pairs or groups (or very formal arrangements set up between individuals on their own). In the middle is *enhanced informal mentoring*, a strategy that falls between the two others.

Instead of a formal program, many organizations choose to implement enhanced informal mentoring. Often this approach is more appropriate for the individuals and cultures. Sometimes that effort leads to a more formal program later.

Here's how it can work. Organizational leaders empower all who are interested to pursue mentoring on their own. Instead of leaving the whole process to chance, however, the leaders provide several kinds of assistance. Here are some examples used by various organizations.

Top executives relay the message (through oral, written, and electronic channels) that they value and support mentoring. They talk freely about their own positive experiences with mentoring and encourage organizational members to pursue it.

Mentoring resource people give a series of presentations on mentoring as part of management training, career self-reliance activities, a conference, brown bag luncheon series, or other events.

The resource team distributes materials on mentoring to those who request them, and extra copies are available in the library or learning center. They place articles and other information about mentoring in the newsletter, other company publications, and on their intranet.

Individuals knowledgeable about mentoring serve as resources to answer questions, encourage individuals, and find additional information that people request. People are referred to resources on the

Internet (such as The Mentoring Group's website, www.mentoringgroup.com).

Supervisors, managers, and other leaders receive training in mentoring theory, behaviors and skills, without necessarily calling themselves mentors.[1] Managers and supervisors are encouraged and rewarded in their performance reviews for implementing mentoring behaviors.

As these individuals become more skilled mentors, they in turn increase the amount of informal, spontaneous mentoring taking place in the organization and often in their community as well.

A good example of mentoring that's somewhere between enhanced informal and the formal end of the continuum is done by the U.S. Department of Agriculture's Natural Resource Conservation Service in California. Outstanding conservationists and individuals in other positions volunteer to be mentors, receive intensive training in mentoring theory and skills, then become available statewide to act as resources and advocates (often by phone) for anyone in the agency who wants their services.

The agency prepared and distributed a videotape showcasing the team of mentors, which increased their visibility and use. By all counts, the planned mentoring effort has been a success.

At the formal end of the continuum are structured programs that recruit, screen, link, train, and monitor pairs (or other combinations such as trios, quartets, groups, and circles) who work together for a set period of time on certain goals. Some ideas for these appear below.

Whichever way you decide to go, carefully consider your role as change agent. Are you appropriate for this role? Ask for feedback from individuals who know. If you are, who else can help you? Definitely use a team or task force to plan and implement the effort.

Mentoring interventions are a great deal of work! The more you do your homework, the better your formal or enhanced informal mentoring will be.

Fortunately, numerous human and other resources are available to help you make decisions and plan your efforts. For a comprehensive look at mentoring in North America and elsewhere, read the materials in the References and Suggested Reading. You'll save yourself time by reading and talking with consultants.

Here are some suggestions to help you design a formal program.

Tips for a Formal Program

Align your efforts with your organization's mission and business needs.

Kram and other experts adamantly stress that you'll waste your time if you don't link the mentoring program to your organization's basic reasons for existing.[2] In other words, as a result of the mentoring effort, the participants will gain skills, knowledge, and attitudes that will allow them to increase their confidence, perform more successfully, and help the organization produce better products and services for its customers or clients. This is true whether you're in a profit-making or not-for-profit organization.

In these days of lean organizations, tight budgets, and increased global competition, organizations must focus on quality, productivity, and efficiency more than before. The human resource development efforts that allow them to meet business goals will be the efforts that aren't only supported—but cheered. Other efforts will be seen as extras and not worth pursuing.

Offer a cafeteria of mentoring options rather than a single choice.

Offer self-paced learning materials, on-line resource sites, orientation sessions, and training workshops that prepare people to enter the continuum of mentoring according to their needs and wishes. In addition to enhanced informal mentoring, consider one or more programs in which mentors and mentees are formally linked.

*Make the mentoring program part of a
larger development effort.*

Your mentoring activities won't do well
if they exist by themselves, apart from
some larger scheme. The more successful
mentoring programs make mentoring an in-
tegral part of leadership or management development, career development, education,
new or transfer employee orientation, or
quality assurance. Surround your mentoring
participants with learning opportunities
that continue to increase their motivation
and skills throughout the program.

Hewlett-Packard Company and its
spin-off, Agilent Technologies, as part of
their accelerated development programs for
promising senior managers, offer mentees
numerous courses and development assignments in addition to relationships with high-
level mentors.

The Federal Executive Development
Program provides an array of classes on
topics that range from computer technology
and managerial productivity to performance
appraisal.

Your mentees should be able to show
how the help they get from their mentors
fits into their overall career development
plans.

Insist that participation in the mentoring initiatives be voluntary.

Keep one firm rule in mind when initiating a mentoring program: ask participants to join on a voluntary basis only, and place no penalties on those who choose not to participate in the first place or withdraw later.[3]
To prevent dropouts, keep commitments relatively short-term, and share a clear statement of expectations before participants join. Make provisions for shifts and transfers to occur among mentors and mentees. Be sure to include a no-fault clause that allows people to exit or get re-matched without stigma.

Keep each pair cycle relatively short.

Six to 12 months is a good length of time for a pair or group to interact. It's long enough for development to occur, and yet it isn't a burdensome commitment for your mentors and mentees to make to one another. Always consider your first round a *pilot effort.*
Be sure to include adequate organizing time prior to the beginning of the first mentoring cycle. Once management is committed, whoever is in charge of coordinating the program needs several weeks to contact consultants who can help, order materials,

publicize the effort, decide on goals, recruit volunteers, match pairs (or groups), organize orientation and training sessions, and design evaluation strategies.

Select mentors and mentees carefully.

Most formal mentoring programs require a nominating procedure and then use the coordinators of the programs or a committee to match mentors and mentees. A few are experimenting with computerized mentor-mentee matching systems.

A significant development over the past 15 years is that mentors and mentees are playing a more direct role in the matching process. In many programs, they study profiles, sometimes interview each other, and rank their preferences.

In some companies, managers nominate mentees after the latter complete an application stating the reasons they believe they're good candidates, what they want to get from the program, and the kind of self-development activities they've pursued during the past year.

Give consideration to the mentors' places on the organization chart as well as the length of time they've been with your organization. Mentoring consultant Suzanne Karl told me about her experience at a Fortune 500 company. At first the company linked new employees immediately after their hiring with very senior mentors. It turned out that the new people were very intimidated by these high-level advisors. They were afraid to ask "dumb" questions.

Karl and her colleagues ended up changing the design and linking new people with mentors who were more like themselves but who had worked there a year or two. After the new hires got their feet wet, about a year later, they were ready to take on the more advanced mentors.[4] You'll have to decide which levels of mentors and mentees are best for your organization.

In some organizations, mentors and mentees are chosen from the same functional area (e.g., planning, marketing, research and development). In others, such as Johnson & Johnson/Lifescan and Kimberly-Clark, mentoring task forces make a special effort to bring mentors and mentees together from different functional areas. Both approaches work, and both have their drawbacks.

Be certain that the mentors have the willingness, expertise, commitment, and time to help the mentees. At the same time, screen mentee candidates carefully to be certain they want and are able to participate fully in the program.

Several organizations use questionnaires and instruments to help screen candidates. Two measures are the Mentoring Style Indicator[5] and the Myers-Briggs Temperament Indicator.

Provide training for mentors and mentees.

Research studies show that programs do much better when mentors and mentees are trained in how to carry out their roles and in mentoring skills. Simply winging it doesn't work.

At the same time, give mentors a great deal of flexibility in how they do their mentoring. Don't ask them to present identical information or utilize the same skills. They won't anyway, and you'll get frustrated if you try to force it. Mentors should tailor mentoring to their mentees and to their own styles.

When organizing your training, work with people who can help you with your design. Trainers can present content in a single session, although some groups appreciate having it spread over at least two meetings, usually with homework and digestion time in between. As part of the training, mentors and mentees need some practical printed materials to help them with their tasks.

In the 1970s and 1980s, many programs were implemented without training the mentees. Coordinators assumed that mentors could guide the way, and mentees would follow. We know now that mentees should manage the relationships, so *they definitely need as much preparation as their mentors, maybe more.*

Here are objectives and content you might include in training mentors and mentees who are very new to the idea of mentoring.[6]

POSSIBLE OBJECTIVES

By the end of the workshop, mentors and mentees will be able to:

- Describe the mentoring program including their responsibilities in it

- Analyze and learn from their own past experiences with mentoring

- Describe a structured process for their partnerships

- Identify and practice critical mentoring skills

- Identify potential challenges and resources for meeting these

- Develop action plans for working with their mentoring partners

Depending on the objectives you finally select, here are some ideas for the content of your training.

POSSIBLE CONTENT

- Introduction (purposes of the mentoring program, how it's supported, participants' commitments and responsibilities)

- Icebreaker

- How Mentoring Fits into Individual and Organizational Success (based on mentoring theory and research)

- Your Past Mentoring Experiences (activity)

- The Process of Mentoring

- Introduction of Critical Mentoring Skills (descriptions, examples, demonstrations, practice)

- Desired Mentee Outcomes/Competencies

- Mentee Development Plans/Activities

- Getting Off to the Right Start (demonstration and practice of mentor-mentee meeting)

- Action Planning

- Summary, Resources, and Next Steps

Consultant Margo Murray[7] and others state that training should produce a negotiated agreement of how and when pairs will proceed and at least the beginnings of development plans for the mentees.

You can train the two groups *separately*. I usually use separate sessions with an overlap period in which the two groups interact. When the groups meet separately, they feel freer to ask questions and express concerns about their roles. During the joint segment, I present content appropriate for both to hear.

You can also train your participants *together*. Many trainers prefer this approach, and it has the advantage of everyone sharing the same learning experience. When combining groups, I always insist on separate break-out sessions for mentors and mentees so they can candidly voice their concerns. (For more ideas, see Phillips-Jones, *The Mentoring Program Design Package*.)

Your mentors and mentees can get ongoing continuing education by visiting our website (www.mentoringgroup.com). Each month, they can read some Tips for Mentors and Tips for Mentees. You'll also see general Ideas about Mentoring, which you can use in your program. You and they can also e-mail us with any questions. Please make your questions specific, since we get so many inquiries.

Be prepared for potential challenges.

Participants in formalized mentoring programs report tremendous satisfaction with their experiences, even though a number note some problem areas or challenges that you, too, may encounter.

Just as informal pairs struggle with time and energy constraints, pairs in programs report the same pressures. Not only do they have to make time to talk to each other, they're expected to participate in program events! It's the coordinator's responsibility to help pairs learn how to maximize their time. Limit the formal group activities, and be certain to make them outstanding when they do occur.

The second biggest problem reported is *fuzziness in expectations* when roles, responsibilities, and goals aren't made crystal clear at the beginning of the program. Take time to list in writing the responsibilities of all parties, including mentees' managers.

If you have to err in one direction, *underestimate* the contributions to be made by the mentors. If mentors decide to add to this minimum, they can negotiate additions with you and their mentees later.

The third challenge is the difficulty mentees have in *selecting objectives to work on* with their mentors. I've found that most mentees struggle with identifying one to three specific objectives or goals for their partnerships. They either set goals that are too large for the timeframe or ones that don't take advantage of the broad or in-depth experience of their mentors.

With your planning group, spend plenty of time identifying potential *mentee outcomes*, usually stated as desired competencies. Various competency domains are available, or you can create your own. Having this list will help your pairs zero in on potential skills on which to work. If your organization has an assessment center, see if you can use the list of competencies on which candidates are tested.

A fourth challenge relates to the *triangles* that occur among mentors, mentees, and the mentees' immediate managers. Many programs run into difficulties because managers aren't included in planning and implementation. As a result, they're sometimes reluctant to release the mentees for mentoring activities, especially when workloads are heavy.

Since these managers are sometimes evaluated by the higher-level mentors, they feel obligated to release the mentees but are frustrated when production is delayed. These problems reflect poorly on the managers and increase the burden on other employees. Some managers express resentment because the mentoring relationships enable mentees to bypass the managers on issues beyond those sanctioned by the formal mentoring program.

Be certain to discuss this potential challenge openly with all three groups. Develop a gameplan which includes alternatives acceptable to everyone. Include mentees' managers in all parts of the program, and give them recognition for their contributions.

Build in a monitoring system.

Evaluate your program carefully from the start. When it comes time to convince decision makers to keep, expand, or drop the mentoring program, you'll have the data you need to make your point.

To do this, build in some checkpoints along the way—meetings, memos or mini-reports, phone calls—to keep your mentors and mentees motivated and to collect the information you need. (Consider hiring an outside group to do this if you're too stretched.)

Try to phone or visit each of your mentors weekly at first then at least monthly to see how things are going and to share news. Ask individual mentors if it's okay to share their ideas with the other mentors. They'll probably be flattered you asked. Keep a log of these calls and anecdotes, and tally your facts and figures from them later.

Near the middle and end of each cycle, require the participants to fill out short evaluation reports on their activities and reactions to the program. Provide copies of a simple form with a due date.

Collect data which show that the mentoring program is making a positive difference in the lives of the participants as well as in the organization. For example, many organizations keep count of all the career progress (skills gained, raises, promotions, transfers, career decisions, progress toward goals from one performance evaluation to the next) made by the participants.

Note attendance, retention, and productivity records to see if you can attribute at least some of the gains to the mentoring efforts. Also note challenges faced. See References and Suggested Reading for additional suggestions to help you evaluate your mentoring.

Planned mentoring can *appear* informal or very formal. Actually, any strategy on the continuum requires careful thought and planning. Determine what's right for your organization.

If you asked me to make one recommendation, it would be that you start small, involve everyone who has a stake in the outcomes, and make sure your initial effort is very successful. It's fairly easy for planned mentoring to expand later if its beginning is a solid success.

Some Gentle Reminders

Not everyone has the skills or the desire to become a mentors' mentor, but if you do, take the challenge! In the process of putting your effort together, be sure to keep track of your own goals. As part of the mentoring cycle, remember that you, too, as a mentors' mentor, are supposed to work yourself out of a job.

Groom your replacement. Develop your mentees so that they can become mentors and keep the program growing and improving. Always be certain that your program enhances the participants' skills, satisfaction, and productivity, and contributes to your organization's major goals.

Planned mentoring initiatives are complex and demand a high level of commitment and time on the part of their champions. *In my opinion, it's better not to start a formal mentoring effort unless you can do it right.*

If you do go ahead, have fun with your project, and be sure your participants have fun, too. It's a way you can make a key difference in *multiple lives.*

13

Closing Thoughts

We bring no consciousness of Community when we deny we ever had mentors, though in truth we did, and we rigorously suppress all mention of their names, in all our public utterances.

—Richard N. Bolles

Still not convinced? Does the idea of gaining or being a mentor still make you uneasy? Consider this. Without a mentor, individuals can suffer negative effects far beyond the obvious area of career development.

Depending on other factors, they can experience lower self-confidence, damaged self-esteem, and even various levels of depression.

As a rule, youths and adults who miss out on emotional support from caring individuals don't thrive and develop as well as those who receive such nurturing. Yale professor Dan Levinson may have been the first to predict that mentor absence can actually have serious emotional consequences.[1]

A man I'll call Don was an attractive, struggling actor when we met. He was on the brink of his 40th birthday and was extremely depressed about his lack of progress. He blamed his failure on the fact that no one had ever taken a real interest in him.

"My parents were more interested in my older sister than me. My first agent never tried to get me bookings. My current one is after my body more than anything else. The casting directors are all prejudiced because I'm too good looking or too tall or too something for their parts. Even in drama school my teachers never spent any extra time with me."

Don knew what mentors were and he expressed bitterness that he was never included in what he called the magic circle.

"All my friends got where they are because they were helped by some older guy. Take Jason. This producer saw him on TV one day and decided he was great. Talk about being in the right place at the right time. I should be so lucky. I hate to sound bitter, but I am. If somebody would just take a chance on me for once, I wouldn't be groveling around here at the bottom. I'd really be somebody by now."

Was Don merely complaining and refusing to take responsibility for his own life? He was definitely contributing to the problem. His skills of interacting with other people were limited. He was a blamer. He made choices about how he reacted to the plate he was given.

However, I believe that his situation would have been dramatically improved if one or more strong mentors had reached out to him, even at this later point in his life.

The very act of reaching out is as valuable as any concrete help mentors have the power to give. I've seen enough evidence to convince me that help from a valued adult has a powerful psychological effect on people of any age.

A woman I'll call Sue, whose father left her and her alcoholic mother when she was two, had a childhood of painful experiences. She and her mother struggled from town to town with barely enough money to make ends meet. Sue's mother was strict, abused her physically and criticized her every move, telling her what to do and refusing to let her make any of her own decisions.

Somehow Sue managed to stay out of trouble and finish high school, but she felt

totally lost after she graduated. She finally
moved out of her mother's apartment and
tried to make it on her own. When we met,
she'd been drifting from job to job and relationship to relationship, and she was confused and frustrated with her life.

She couldn't say one good word about
herself and didn't believe anyone would ever
care for her. In her own words: "I'd like to
think there was someone out there who
could really care about me and help me get
my life together. Some chance!"

If Don and Sue had the right mentors
earlier in their lives to assist them with
their goals and to help them in the youth-to-
adult development process, I believe they
would have viewed themselves and their
success possibilities much differently.

Don's refusal to take much responsibility for himself makes one wonder if even
a powerful, dedicated mentor could totally
turn around his negative self-image and
world view. Yet, chances are excellent that
such an experience could have positive
effects on him even at this point in his life.

Sue's mother probably cared about her
but didn't know how to translate that caring
into actions that helped Sue's development.
Fortunately, Sue had a second chance.

As Sue's psychologist, I worked to be
the mentor she needed in order to provide a
bridge from her childhood dependence on
adults into a more adult life role. I'm happy

to report that she finally landed a job she loves and feels much better about herself and about the potentially long-term relationships she's now forming with others.

I could report hundreds of stories like Sue's. I don't believe my counseling skills are all that wondrous, but I do believe my presence and my genuine interest and encouragement have helped. I like to think God is working through me and many, many other mentors to give individuals a second or third chance.

It can be risky to place your trust in a mentor, and it's sometimes even riskier to act as a mentor to others. It's tempting to skip these involvements altogether. Yet, despite the time it takes, the mistakes we all make, and the pain that some partings can evoke, *the relationships are worth it.*

I encourage you to go out on that limb from time to time. Don't wait around and wonder how far you can go without a mentor's help. Just do your homework first.

Don't overlook a promising mentee and assume that someone else will come along to help. You could be only person that sees his or her potential.

One of the favorite books of career counselors is the *Dictionary of Occupational Titles* published by the U.S. Department of Labor. The 40,000 or so jobs in the U.S. are listed under three categories according to whether the job deals mainly with people, ideas or data, or things. Within each group, the types of work done are ranked according to their importance and difficulty.

Under the people jobs, the *highest, most complex and important skill is mentoring,* doing what it takes to help others reach their critical life goals.

I hope you've enjoyed remembering all these important people in your life. Chances are good that your mentors and mentees have the same recollections of you. I also hope you'll risk a few more of these relationships in the years you have left.

Notes

Chapter 1.

1. Johnston, W.B. & H.A. Packer (1987) *Workforce 2000: Work and Workers for the 21st Century*. Indianapolis: Hudson Institute.

2. By May 1999, General Powell's America's Promise had reached more than 10 million children. Source: PricewaterhouseCoopers measurement study press release, May 17, 1999.

3. "Cross-difference mentoring" is a term I coined to cover mentoring between persons who differ from each other in age, gender, culture, style, geography, or other key characteristics.

4. My original research on mentoring was the basis for my 1977 UCLA doctoral dissertation, *"Mentors and Proteges: A Study of the Career Development of Women Managers and Executives in Business and Industry."* The study included written surveys and/or interviews with 332 women listed by Standard and Poors or *Business Week* magazine who met certain success criteria.

Chapter 2.

1. Packard, David, *The HP Way: How Bill Hewlett and I Built Our Company.* See References.

2. Jane Evans was listed as one of *Business Week's* Top 100 Women in 1977. Personal interview.

3. Mead, Margaret, *Blackberry Winter: My Earlier Years.* See References.

4. George Bull (1998) *Michelangeo: A Biography.* Torrance, Calif.: Griffin Publishing Group.

5. Dr. Daniel Levinson, personal interview.

Chapter 3.

1. James M. Kouzes & Barry Z. Posner provide numerous practical examples of how to inspire and encourage people. See their book, *Encouraging the Heart*, listed in References.

2. Rosenthal, Robert & Lenore Jacobsen, *Pygmalian in the Classroom.* See References.

3. Roazen, Paul, *Freud and His Followers.* See References.

4. This study was part of my doctoral research at UCLA in 1976 and 1977.

5. Jean Parvin described Bill Walsh's relationship with Paul Brown in "Someone to Watch over You," *Reader's Digest*, September 1992.

6. I've concluded that the protege or mentee is the one to decide if someone is his or her mentor. I'm careful when I attribute the word mentor or mentoring to any pair. I assume that many of the coaches Walsh developed over the years would call Walsh their "mentor," but since I haven't interviewed them I'll say that it looks like mentoring from my vantage point.

7. Dr. Albert Bandura has been the major pioneer in the areas of Social Learning Theory and Self Efficacy. In a nutshell, Bandura says that we learn from watching social models and the consequences they receive. Our self-efficacy (belief in our capability to successfully accomplish tasks) increases when we receive positive reinforcement from respected models, recognize we can perform well like they do, and successfully complete "mastery experiences"—hard tasks that allow us to stretch and increase our skills.

8. Wooden, John, *They Call Me Coach*. See References.

9. Cheryl Tiegs mentioned these mentors in her remarks to the Clairol mentors and mentees. I provided the training orientations for the participants for six years. Actor and businessperson Linda Evans, who was the chairperson for the first five years, named Barbara Stanwick as her mentor.

10. Cuomo, Matilda R. (Ed.), *The Person Who Changed my Life: Prominent Americans Recall their Mentors.* See References.

11. Carter, Jimmy, *Why Not the Best?* See References.

12. Cavett, Dick, *Cavett.* New York: See References.

Chapter 4.

1. Mead, Margaret, *Blackberry Winter*, page 138. See References.

2. Roazen, Paul, *Freud and His Followers.* See References.

3. Eugene Jennings wrote about "crucial subordinates" in *Routes to the Executive Suite* (1971) New York: McGraw-Hill. His classic book contains numerous fascinating stories of high-level pairs who zigzagged together

through the top echelons of American business.

4. Barth, John (1972) *Chimera*. New York: Random House.

5. Kantor, Rosabeth, *Men and Women of the Corporation*. See References.

6. Erikson, Erik, Identity and the Life Cycle. *Psychological Issues*. Also *Childhood and Society*, 2nd ed. See References.

Chapter 5.

1. Clawson, James G. & M.B. Blank, What Really Counts in Superior-Subordinate Relationships? Lessons from Business. *Mentoring International*. See References.

2. Morgan W. McCall emphasizes that one of the most important skills for personal growth is "learning how to create a learning environment wherever you are . . . Treat people in ways that make them want to coach you, support you, give you feedback, and allow you to make mistakes."

3. Personal communication with Dr. Roger Gould, a member of my dissertation committee.

4. Thompson, Gene W. & Paul H. Dalton, Are R&D Organizations Obsolete? *Harvard Business Review*. See References.

Chapter 6.

1. My original research in 1976 focused on females, most of whom stayed for years in their organizations.

2. Eugene Jennings used the term "organization sponsors" in *Routes to the Executive Suite.* I assume he coined it, and it's used here to describe a type of mentor found at high levels of organizations. Many resist the idea that such persons exist in modern corporations, but my experience is that they do.

3. *New Yorker*, August 1, 1977.

4. Kronenberger, L. (Ed.), *Brief Lives: A Biographical Companion to the Arts,* p. 87. See References.

5. Many people debate as to whether or not "peer mentors" are actual mentors. To me, they are if they fit the original definition (help a mentee set goals and build skills to achieve them). Dr. Beverly Kaye speaks and writes about "mentworking," which is *simultaneously* finding new mentors for oneself and mentoring others. She emphasizes the value

and practicality of learning and teaching at
the same time. (Personal communication)

6. Davenport, Marcia, *Mozart*. See References.

7. Matilda R. Cuomo, *The Person Who Changed
my Life*, pages 83 and 84.

8. Hakim, Cliff, *We Are All Self Employed*. See
References.

9. Cliff Hakim, personal communication.

Chapter 7.

1. For a copy of the 16-page booklet,
*"Strategies for Getting the Mentoring You
Need: A Look at Best Practices of Successful
Mentees,"* send $4US to CCC/The Mentoring
Group, 13560 Mesa Drive, Grass Valley, CA
95949. Clearly print your name and address. If
you prefer, phone (530) 268-1146 and charge it
to a Visa or Mastercard number.

Chapter 8.

1. I dubbed these unofficial mentoring rules of
behavior "the new mentoring etiquette" in
1993. Since then, The Mentoring Group has
had many requests for reprints. You have
permission to copy this chapter for distribu-

tion to your participants as long as you give
credit to CCC/The Mentoring Group.

Chapter 9.

1. These are the stages I identified in my 1977
dissertation research.

2. Psychiatrist Roger Gould helped me define
the concept of "psychological disengagement"
in mentoring. He emphasized that a mentor
and mentee could remain geographically or
physically close. Healthy psychological disengagement requires an emotional separation.

3. Levinson, D.J., Darrow, C.M., Klein, E.B.,
Levinson, M.H., & McKee, B. (1976) Periods in
the Adult Development of Men: Ages 18 to 45.
The Counseling Psychologist, 6 (1).

4. Berg, A. Scott, *Max Perkins: Editor of
Genius*: See References.

5. Svengali was a character in the book,
Trilby, by George Du Maurier. A manipulative
musician-tutor, Svengali used hypnosis in an
abusive way to control his female pupil
Trilby. According to *Webster's Ninth New
Collegiate Dictionary*, a Svengali is "one who
attempts, usually with evil intentions, to per-
suade or force another to do his bidding."

6. Berg, A. Scott, *Max Perkins: Editor of Genius*: See References.

7. Roazen, Paul, *Freud and His Followers*.

8. Roazen, Paul, *Freud and His Followers*.

Chapter 10.

1. Personal communication with Roz Loring at UCLA.

2. Cognitive restructuring is the term used by Dr. David Burn in his book, *The New Mood Therapy*. In essence, it's recognizing negative thought patterns and stopping them or replacing them with positive (although realistic) patterns.

3. Personal communication with Dr. Levinson.

4. Berg, A. Scott, *Max Perkins: Editor of Genius*. See References.

5. Sheehy, Gail, *Passages*, page 132. See References.

Chapter 11.

1. The Mentoring Skills Assessment (MSA) is available from MindGarden, 1690 Woodside

Road, Redwood City, CA 94061, (650) 261-3500.
The MSA contains separate 360º assessments
for mentees and mentors.

Chapter 12.

1. Managers can benefit from the booklet,
*"What Every Manager Should Know about
Mentoring: Your Three Roles to Help
Employees Excel."* For a copy of the 12-page
booklet, send $4US to CCC/The Mentoring
Group, 13560 Mesa Drive, Grass Valley, CA
95949. Clearly print your name and address. If
you prefer, phone (530) 268-1146 and charge it
to a Visa or Mastercard number.

2. Kram, Kathy, *Mentoring at Work: Developmental Relationships in Organizational Life.*
See References.

3. The one exception to the voluntary rule can
be new hires. Most are anxious to learn about
the organization and don't mind being assigned
to mentors and programs. However, even new
hires should have the opportunity to opt out
of mentoring partnerships or programs if they
have acceptable reasons.

4. Personal communication with consultant
Suzie Karl.

5. For information on the *Mentoring Style Indicator*, contact Dr. William and Marilynne Gray, The Mentoring Institute. See References.

6. For more information, see *The Mentoring Program Coordinator's Guide* in References.

7. Murray, Margo, *Beyond The Myths and Magic of Mentoring: How to Facilitate an Effective Mentoring Program*. See References.

Chapter 13.

1. Personal communication with Dr. Levinson.

References and Suggested Reading

Alleman, E. (1986) Measuring Mentoring: Frequency, Quality, Impact in *Mentoring: Aid to Excellence in Career Development, Business and the Professions*. (Gray, W.A. & M.M. Gray, eds.) Sidney, B.C.: International Association for Mentoring.

Alleman, E. & W.A. Gray *Design Productive Mentoring Programs*. Alexandria, VA.: ASTD Info-Line No. 609.

Bell, C.R. (1996) *Managers as Mentors: Building Partnerships for Learning*. San Francisco: Berrett-Koehler Publishers.

Carter, J. (1975) *Why Not the Best?* Nashville: Broadman Press.

Cavett, D. & C. Porterfield (1974) *Cavett*. New York: Harcourt, Brace, Jovanovich (Bantam edition, 1975).

Clawson, J.G. & M.B. Blank (1990) What Really Counts in Superior-Subordinate Relationships? Lessons from Business. *Mentoring International*, 4, 12-16.

Clawson, J.G. & K.E. Kram (1984) Managing Cross-Gender Mentoring. *Business Horizons*, 27, 3, 22-32.

Collins, E.G. & P. Scott (1978) Everyone Who Makes It Has a Mentor. *Harvard Business Review*, July-August, 89-101.

Covey, S. (1989) *The Seven Habits of Highly Effective People*. New York: Simon & Schuster.

Cuomo, M.R. (Ed.) (1999) *The Person Who Changed my Life: Prominent Americans Recall their Mentors*. Secaucus, N.J.: Carol Publishing Group.

Davenport, M. (1932) *Mozart*. New York: Charles Scribner (Avon Books edition, 1979).

Erikson, E.H. (1959) Identity and the Life Cycle. *Psychological Issues*, 1, 1.

Erikson, E.H. (1963) *Childhood and Society*, 2nd ed. New York: W.W. Norton.

Funke, L. & J.E. Booth (1961) *Actors Talk about Acting*. New York: Avon Books.

Geiger, A.H. (1992) Measures for Mentors. *Training and Development*, 46, 2, 65-67.

Gould, R.L. (1978) *Transformations: Growth and Change in Adult Life.* New York: Simon & Schuster.

Gray, W.A. (1989) Situational Mentoring: Custom Designed Planned Mentoring Programs. *Mentoring International*, 3, 1, 19-28.

Gray, W.A.; M.M. Gray; & T.D. Anderson, (1991) *Mentoring Style Indicator.* Vancouver, B.C.: International Centre for Mentoring.

Hakim, C. (1994) *We Are All Self-Employed: The New Social Contract for Working in a Changed World.* San Francisco: Berrett-Koehler Publishers.

Jung, C.G. (1960) The Stages of Life. *The Collected Works: Structure and Dynamics of the Psyche,* Vol. 8. Translated by R.F.C. Hill. New York: Panthean.

Kanter, R.M. (1977) *Men & Women of the Corporation.* New York: Basic Books.

Kouzes, J.M. & B.Z. Posner (1999) *Encouraging the Heart: A Leader's Guide to Rewarding and Recognizing Others.* San Francisco: Jossey-Bass.

Kouzes, J.M. & B.Z. Posner (1987) *The Leadership Challenge: How to Get Extra-*

ordinary Things Done in Organizations. San Francisco: Jossey-Bass.

Kram, K.E. (1996) Mentoring and Leadership Development, *Journal of Leadership and Organizational Development,* Vol. 17(3), 4-5.

Kram, K.E. (1988) *Mentoring at Work: Developmental Relationships in Organizational Life.* Lanham, Md.: University Press of America.

Kram, K.E. (1983) Phases of the Mentor Relationship. *Academy of Management Journal,* 26, 4, 608-625.

Kram, K.E. (1980) *Mentoring Processes at Work.* Unpublished doctoral dissertation, Yale University, New Haven.

Kronenberger, L. (Ed.) (1971) *Brief Lives: A Biographical Companion to the Arts.* Boston: Little, Brown and Company, Atlantic Monthly Press.

Levinson, D.J.; C.M. Darrow; E.B. Klein; M.H. Levinson; & B. McKee (1976) Periods in the Adult Development of Men: Ages 18 to 45. *The Counseling Psychologist,* 6, 1, 21-25.

Levinson, D.J. et al (1985) *Seasons of a Man's Life.* New York: Knopf.

McCall, M.W. Jr. (1998) *High Flyers: Developing the Next Generation of Leaders.* Boston: Harvard Business School Press.

Mead, M. (1972) *Blackberry Winter: My Earlier Years.* New York: William Morrow.

Murray, M. with M.A. Owen (1991) *Beyond the Myths and Magic of Mentoring: How to Facilitate an Effective Mentoring Program.* San Francisco: Jossey-Bass.

Packard, D. (1995) *The HP Way: How Bill Hewlett and I Built Our Company.* New York: Harper Collins.

Parvin, J. (1992) Someone to Watch Over You. *Reader's Digest,* September, 127-130.

Phillips-Jones, L. (2000, 1996) *The Mentoring Program Design Package* (The Mentoring Program Coordinator's Guide, The Mentor's Guide, The Mentee's Guide). Grass Valley, Calif.: Coalition of Counseling Centers/The Mentoring Group.

Phillips-Jones, L. (1998) *75 Things to Do with your Mentees: Practical and Effective Development Ideas You can Try.* Grass Valley, Calif.: Coalition of Counseling Centers/The Mentoring Group.

Phillips-Jones, L. (1997 and 1993 updates) *The New Mentors and Proteges: How to Succeed with the New Mentoring Partnerships.* Grass Valley, Calif.: Coalition of Counseling Centers/The Mentoring Group.

Phillips-Jones, L. (1997) *What Every Manager should Know about Mentoring: Your Three Mentoring Roles to Help Employees Excel.* Grass Valley, Calif.: Coalition of Counseling Centers/The Mentoring Group.

Phillips-Jones, L. (2000) *Strategies for Getting the Mentoring You Need: A Look at Best Practices of Successful Mentees.* Grass Valley, Calif.: Coalition of Counseling Centers/The Mentoring Group.

Phillips-Jones, L. (1990) Common Problems in Mentoring Relationships in (Frantzreb, R., Ed.) *Training and Development Yearbook.* Englewood Cliffs, N.J.: Prentice Hall.

Phillips-Jones, L. (1983) Establishing a Formalized Mentoring Program. *Training and Development Journal,* 37, 48-52.

Phillips-Jones, L. (1982) *Mentors and Proteges: How to Establish, Strengthen and Get the Most from a Mentor-Protege Relationship.* New York: Arbor House.

Phillips, L. (1977) *Mentors and Proteges: A Study of the Career Development of Women Managers and Executives in Business and Industry.* Unpublished doctoral dissertation, University of California, Los Angeles.

Roazen, P. (1974) *Freud and His Followers.* New York: New American Library, A Meridian Book.

Rosenthal, R. & L. Jacobson (1968) *Pygmalian in the Classroom.* New York: Holt, Rinehart and Winston.

Senge, P.M.; A. Kleiner; & C. Roberts (1994) *The Fifth Discipline Fieldbook: Strategies and Tools for Building a Learning Organization.* New York: Currency Doubleday.

Senge, P.M. (1990) *The Fifth Discipline: The Art & Practice of the Learning Organization.* New York: Currency Doubleday.

Sheehy, G. (1974) *Passages: Predictable Crises of Adult Life.* New York: E.P. Dutton.

Sheehy, G. (1976) The Mentor Connection: The Secret Link in the Successful Woman's Life. *New York*, April 5, 33-39.

Tannen, D. (1994) *Talking from 9 to 5: Women and Men in the Workplace: Language, Sex and Power.* New York: Avon Books.

Thompson, P.H. & G.W. Dalton (1976) Are R&D Organizations Obsolete? *Harvard Business Review,* November-December, 105-116.

Wooden, J. (1972) *They Call Me Coach.* Waco, Tex.: Word Books (Bantam Books edition, 1973).

Zey, M.G. (1984) *The Mentor Connection.* Homewood, Ill.: Dow Jones-Irwin.

The Author

Dr. Linda Phillips-Jones is a licensed psychologist, consultant, researcher, and author. She helps businesses, professional associations, government agencies, and other organizations design, implement, and evaluate mentoring programs.

Dr. Phillips-Jones received a Ph.D. in counseling psychology from UCLA, master's degree from Stanford University, and bachelor's from the University of Nevada-Reno.

Her 1977 doctoral dissertation on the subject of mentoring was probably the first on the topic. Since then, several hundred mentoring dissertations and theses have been written, most referring to this original work. Her first book on mentoring, *Mentors and Proteges: How to Establish, Strengthen and Get the Most from a Mentor-Protege Relationship* (Arbor House, 1982), has been used worldwide.

The Mentoring Group's training materials have been used by Hewlett-Packard, Agilent Technologies, Abbott Laboratories, Ameritech, FedEx, Conoco, HBO, MTV, GTE, Alyeska Pipeline Service Company, Eli Lilly, Southwest Airlines, AT&T, Fluor Daniel, Harley Davidson, Southwest Bell, Clairol, Enron, Starbucks, PricewaterhouseCoopers LLP, UPS, Lucent Technologies, Andersen

Consulting, DuPont, U.S. Cellular, State Farm
Insurance, Space Systems/Loral, American
Family Insurance, Farmer's Insurance, Kimberly-Clark, numerous colleges, universities,
and school districts, plus many federal and
state governments and provinces. She's the
author of the Mentoring Skills Assessment
(MSA), published by MindGarden, Redwood
City, California.

Dr. Phillips-Jones has been quoted *in
The Wall Street Journal, USA Today, News-
day, The Los Angeles Times, The Boston
Globe, Success, Psychology Today, Glamour,
New Woman, Executive Female, Training and
Development Journal, Reader's Digest, Entre-
preneur,* and numerous other periodicals.

She's featured as a mentoring expert in
the following videos: "Building Bridges: How
to Build a Powerful Network," produced by
the National Association of Female Executives; "Mentoring that Makes a Difference: For
Mentors"; "Mentoring that Makes a Difference:
For Mentees"; and "Mentoring: The Success
Connection."

Dr. Phillips-Jones was invited to Hungary to teach mentoring as part of an entre-
preneurial development program of the U.S.
Department of Labor and the Women's Economic Alliance Foundation in Washington. She
and her psychologist husband, Dr. G. Brian
Jones, were invited as foreign experts to teach
managerial psychology and organizational behavior in the People's Republic of China and

Kenya. She's conducted in-person mentoring workshops in Canada, Scotland, Germany, Australia, Malaysia, and Hong Kong and on-line training via the Internet in many other countries.

During the Vietnam War, she worked five years as a teacher trainer and curriculum designer in South Vietnam.